The Pampered Chef®
Casual Cooking
Easy Recipes for Indoors and Out

When the weather turns warm, our attention naturally shifts to making fun, flavorful and fresh food in a relaxed atmosphere. In *Casual Cooking*, we begin with mouthwatering recipes that capture the spirit of American cooking — the backyard barbecue. Sizzling steaks, juicy burgers and smoky ribs are accompanied by a collection of traditional side dishes that represent some of the best of our culinary heritage. To complement these outdoor classics, we've created an impressive chapter of fast, fabulous indoor recipes designed to take advantage of summer's best produce while featuring cooking techniques that will keep your kitchen cool. And of course, we haven't forgotten those delightful desserts that are sure to round out any type of family meal you prefer.

Whether it's a casual gathering of friends or a simple family supper, you'll find yourself turning these pages again and again for inspiration. All of the recipes in this cookbook have been developed, tested and tasted in The Pampered Chef Test Kitchens with foolproof results that will delight your family and friends. The tips, techniques and menu suggestions we've included with each beautifully photographed recipe will help you bring dinner to the table with a smile — guaranteed.

With high-quality kitchen tools and terrific recipes from The Pampered Chef, we hope *Casual Cooking* will become an expression of your lifestyle, now and all year long.

Enjoy!

The Pampered Chef Test Kitchens

On the cover: Cajun Chicken Salad (p. 23), Grilled Garlic Bread (p. 25), Minted Melon Medley (p. 37)

The Pampered Chef is the premier direct-seller of high-quality kitchen tools sold through in-home Kitchen Shows. Founded in 1980 by educator and home economist Doris Christopher, and headquartered in Addison, Illinois, The Pampered Chef is committed to enhancing family life by providing quality kitchen products supported by superior service and information.

Contents

The Great Outdoors 4

Nothing compares to the pleasures of preparing food in the open air — the aroma and smoky flavor of foods cooked on the grill are simply irresistible. Grilling is fun, convenient, and a great way to turn any meal into a special event. Here we offer a full range of exceptional grilled recipes such as *South-of-the-Border Steaks*, *Citrus Shrimp Skewers* and *Cajun Chicken Salad*. Pair these hot-off-the-grill entrées with spectacular picnic sides like *Corn on the Cob with Herb Butters* and *Calico Coleslaw* and you'll have a summertime meal perfect for enjoying around the patio or dining room table. You'll find our simple sauces, marinades and seasoning mixes add variety and flavor to many of your grilled favorites. And, we'll help you discover secrets for successful grilling with tips, tools and techniques guaranteed to make you a backyard cooking hero. So, fire up the grill and get ready for great results!

Mexican Burger Bar (p. 29)

Cool Kitchen Cooking 54

When you just can't bear to turn on the oven, turn to The Pampered Chef for delectable warm weather solutions. Our hearty sandwiches, satisfying salads and sizzling stovetop suppers are a breeze to make, and most require little cooking. Prepare delicious fast food with updated favorites like *Taco-Topped Potatoes* and *Pepperoni Pizzadillas*. Create your own carryout cuisine with our quality cookware and ethnic-inspired skillet dishes including *Sweet & Sour Shrimp Stir-Fry*, *Curried Vegetable Couscous* or *Italian Chicken Pasta Toss*. Discover how grill pan cooking can bring the intriguing flavor of outdoor grilling indoors with enticing recipes for meats, fish, poultry and more. You'll stay cool, calm and collected on the warmest of days with these easy, quick-cooked meals that will keep kitchen heat to a minimum and family enjoyment to a maximum.

Curried Vegetable Couscous (p. 87)

Sweet Sensations 96

Like a tall glass of lemonade on a hot summer day, these recipes will satisfy your desire for quick, easy and refreshing summertime treats. We've got the scoop on creating easy, make-ahead ice cream pies, parfaits and dessert pizzas. Our ice-cold beverages like *Wild Raspberry Summer Sipper* are certain to cool you off. Those just-picked farm stand fruits are put to luscious use in quick desserts such as *Fresh Strawberry Pie* and *Apple Berry Crisp*. And, casual summer elegance is here to stay with irresistible *Lemon Blueberry Cheesecake Torte*. So for a frosty, fresh or fabulous finish to any family meal or special occasion, we invite you to choose your favorites from our inviting dessert collection.

Hawaiian Dessert Cloud (p. 109)

The Great Outdoors

Fire up the grill for

irresistible entrées paired

with sensational

summer sides.

South-of-the-Border Steaks (p. 6),
Corn on the Cob with Herb Butters (p. 7)

South-of-the-Border Steaks

Prep time: 15 minutes   Grill time: 15-18 minutes

Fire up the grill for a weeknight fiesta showcasing these tender, juicy steaks. (Pictured on p. 4-5)

▲ Beef top loin steak
is also known as strip
steak, New York or
Kansas City strip steak,
or Delmonico steak.

▲ Substitute one
1½-pound boneless
beef top sirloin steak,
cut 1 inch thick, for
boneless beef top loin
steaks. Grill, uncovered,
17-21 minutes for
medium rare (145°F)
to medium (160°F)
doneness, turning
occasionally.

▲ Snipped fresh parsley
can be substituted for
cilantro, if desired.

1   **small tomato, chopped (¾ cup)**
¼   **cup snipped fresh cilantro**
1   **lime**
½   **cup (2 ounces) shredded Mexican cheese blend, divided**
1   **teaspoon *Pantry Southwestern Seasoning* Mix**
2   **garlic cloves, pressed**
½   **teaspoon salt**
2   **boneless beef top loin steaks, cut 1 inch thick (about 1½ pounds)**

1. Prepare grill for direct cooking over medium coals. Chop tomato with **Utility Knife**. Snip cilantro using **Kitchen Shears**. Juice lime with **Juicer** to measure 1 teaspoon juice. Combine tomato, cilantro, juice, ¼ cup of the cheese and seasoning mix in **Small Batter Bowl**; mix gently and set aside.

2. Combine garlic pressed with **Garlic Press** and salt in small bowl. Using **Small Spreader**, spread garlic mixture evenly over both sides of steaks.

3. Place steaks on grid of grill. Grill, uncovered, 15-18 minutes for medium rare (145°F) to medium (160°F) doneness, turning occasionally using **Barbecue Turner**. About 2 minutes before steaks are done, remove from grill to **Oval Carving Platter Set**; top evenly with tomato mixture and sprinkle with remaining cheese. Return steaks to grill; cover. Continue cooking until steaks reach desired doneness and cheese is melted.

4. Remove steaks to platter set using barbecue turner. Cut into servings using **Carving Set**.

Yield: 4 servings

Nutrients per serving: Calories 310, Total Fat 14 g, Saturated Fat 4 g, Cholesterol 125 mg, Carbohydrate 2 g, Protein 42 g, Sodium 490 mg, Fiber 0 g

Diabetic exchanges per serving: ½ vegetable, 5½ meat

MENU SUGGESTION

For a festive meal, pair these zesty steaks with *Corn on the Cob with Cilantro-Lime Butter* (p. 7) and grilled potatoes (p. 49). Cool down with *Iced Coffee Latte* (p. 101).

Corn on the Cob with Herb Butters

Prep time: 10 minutes   Cook time: 30 minutes   Chill time: 30 minutes

Dress up corn to match just about any main dish with a variety of herbs and our unique Seasoning Mixes. (Pictured on p. 4-5)

Cilantro-Lime Butter

- ¼ **cup butter or margarine, softened**
- 1 **lime**
- 1 **teaspoon finely snipped fresh cilantro**
- ¼ **teaspoon salt**

Corn

- 6 **ears corn, husks and silk removed**

1. For cilantro-lime butter, place butter in **Small Batter Bowl**. Zest lime using **Lemon Zester/Scorer**; finely chop zest using **Chef's Knife** to measure 1 teaspoon zest. Juice lime to measure 1 teaspoon juice. Finely snip cilantro with **Kitchen Shears**. Add zest, juice, cilantro and salt to softened butter; mix well using **Skinny Scraper**. Fill **Corn Butterer** with butter mixture; refrigerate 30 minutes.

2. For corn, bring 4 quarts water to a boil in covered **Professional (8-qt.) Stockpot** over high heat. Trim ends from ears of corn using chef's knife. Firmly twist **Corn Cob Nobs®** into ears. Carefully add corn to boiling water using **Nylon Tongs**. Cover; return water to a boil. Turn off heat and let corn stand, covered, 8-10 minutes or until crisp-tender. Remove corn and serve immediately with butter.

Yield: 6 servings

Nutrients per serving: Calories 160, Total Fat 9 g, Saturated Fat 5 g, Cholesterol 20 mg, Carbohydrate 21 g, Protein 3 g, Sodium 190 mg, Fiber 2 g

Diabetic exchanges per serving: 1 starch, 2 fat (1 carb)

Variations: *Cajun Butter*: Combine ¼ cup softened butter or margarine, 1 teaspoon **Pantry Cajun Herb Seasoning Mix** and ¼ teaspoon salt. Proceed as recipe directs.

Dill-Lemon Butter: Combine ¼ cup softened butter or margarine, 1 teaspoon **Pantry All-Purpose Dill Mix**, ½ teaspoon finely chopped lemon zest and ¼ teaspoon salt. Proceed as recipe directs.

Lemon Pepper-Parsley Butter: Combine ¼ cup softened butter or margarine, 1 teaspoon **Pantry Lemon Pepper Seasoning Mix**, 1 teaspoon finely snipped fresh parsley and ¼ teaspoon salt. Proceed as recipe directs.

Southwestern Butter: Combine ¼ cup softened butter or margarine, 1 teaspoon **Pantry Southwestern Seasoning Mix** and ¼ teaspoon salt. Proceed as recipe directs.

Tomato-Basil Butter: Combine ¼ cup softened butter or margarine, 1 tablespoon finely chopped sun-dried tomatoes packed in oil (drained and patted dry on paper towels), 1 teaspoon finely snipped fresh basil leaves and ¼ teaspoon garlic salt. Proceed as recipe directs.

Cook's Tips

▲ Herb butters can be prepared up to several days in advance.

▲ To soften butter, microwave butter on 30% power for 15-20 seconds or just until softened.

▲ Corn is most flavorful when eaten as soon after it's picked as possible. Always husk ears and remove the silk just before cooking. Cooking time will vary depending on the variety and age of the corn.

▲ The see-through glass lid to our covered stockpot allows you to easily see when the water returns to a boil. Cooking in a covered stockpot lets steam cook the portions of the ears that are not submerged.

Teriyaki Pork Kebabs with Asian Rice

Prep time: 40 minutes   Marinate time: 30 minutes   Grill time: 14-16 minutes

Nestled on a bed of flavorful rice, these kebabs make a satisfying main dish.

Marinade and Kebabs

- ½ **cup reduced-sodium soy sauce**
- ⅓ **cup packed brown sugar**
- 1 **tablespoon finely chopped, peeled fresh gingerroot**
- 2 **garlic cloves, pressed**
- 2 **teaspoons dark sesame oil**
- 2 **pork tenderloins (about 1 pound each)**
- 1 **medium green bell pepper**
- 1 **medium red bell pepper**
- 3 **fresh pineapple slices, cut 1 inch thick**

Asian Rice

- 1 **can (14½ ounces) reduced-sodium chicken broth**
- 1⅔ **cups water**
- 1 **tablespoon butter or margarine**
- 2 **teaspoons Pantry Asian Seasoning Mix**
- 1½ **cups uncooked converted or long grain rice**
- ⅓ **cup sliced green onions with tops**

1. For marinade, combine soy sauce and brown sugar in **Classic Batter Bowl**. Finely chop gingerroot using **Food Chopper**. Add gingerroot, garlic pressed with **Garlic Press** and oil to batter bowl; mix well. Reserve ½ cup of the marinade; set aside. For kebabs, cut pork into twenty-four 1¼-inch pieces. Add pork to remaining marinade in batter bowl, tossing to coat. Cover; refrigerate 30 minutes.

2. Meanwhile, cut bell peppers into twenty-four 1-inch pieces. Cut pineapple into quarters to make 12 pieces. Prepare grill for direct cooking over medium coals.

3. Remove pork from marinade; discard marinade in batter bowl. Alternately thread pork, bell pepper and pineapple onto six 12-inch skewers. Place kebabs on grid of grill; brush with some of the reserved marinade using **Barbecue Basting Brush**. Grill, uncovered, 14-16 minutes or until pork is no longer pink, turning occasionally with **Barbecue Tongs** and brushing with marinade. Discard any remaining marinade.

4. Meanwhile, for Asian rice, bring chicken broth and water to a boil in **Medium (3-qt.) Saucepan**. Add butter and seasoning mix. Stir in rice. Reduce heat, cover and simmer 20 minutes. Remove from heat; stir in green onions. Let stand 5 minutes.

Yield: 6 servings

Nutrients per serving (1 kebab, 1 cup rice): Calories 610, Total Fat 16 g, Saturated Fat 6 g, Cholesterol 145 mg, Carbohydrate 60 g, Protein 52 g, Sodium 1080 mg, Fiber 1 g

Diabetic exchanges per serving (1 kebab, 1 cup rice): 4 starch, 5 meat

Variation: *Teriyaki Chicken Kebabs:* Substitute 6 boneless, skinless chicken breast halves for the pork tenderloin. Cut chicken lengthwise into thin strips and add to marinade in bowl. Cover; refrigerate 1 hour. Weave chicken, along with bell pepper and pineapple, onto skewers. Grill, uncovered, 10-12 minutes or until chicken is no longer pink, turning occasionally and brushing with marinade.

Cook's Tips

▲ The pork should be marinated for no longer than 30 minutes or the texture will be soft and mushy.

▲ When grilling kebabs, make sure the pieces of meat and vegetables are the same size to ensure even cooking.

▲ Gingerroot has a paper-thin, tan-colored skin that should be removed before use. Store gingerroot in a resealable plastic food storage bag in the refrigerator for up to 3 weeks or in the freezer for up to 6 months. To use frozen gingerroot, just slice off as much as you need.

▲ Already peeled and cored fresh pineapple is available in the produce department in most large supermarkets.

Cook's Tips

▲ Two Cornish hens (about 1¼-1½ pounds each) can be substituted for the chicken. To prepare hens, rinse and pat dry with paper towels. Remove backbone by cutting on either side with kitchen shears. Lay hen flat and cut in between breasts to separate into halves. Repeat with second hen. Marinate and grill as directed 30-35 minutes or until hen registers 170°F in thickest part of breast portion and juices run clear.

▲ Use the instant-read **Pocket Thermometer** or **Digital Thermometer** to accurately check the temperature of the chicken for doneness.

MENU SUGGESTION

Grilled tomatoes (p. 49), hot cooked rice with snipped fresh parsley and breadsticks would be great side dishes for this chicken.

Lemon Chicken with Cucumber Salsa

Prep time: 15 minutes   Marinate time: 2-4 hours   Grill time: 45-50 minutes

A cool cucumber salsa is a colorful and refreshing accompaniment for lemony grilled chicken.

Chicken and Marinade

- 1 **broiler-fryer chicken (4 pounds), cut into quarters**
- 2 **lemons**
- 3 **garlic cloves, pressed**
- 2 **tablespoons olive oil**
- 2 **teaspoons dried oregano leaves**
- 1 **teaspoon paprika**
- ½ **teaspoon salt**
- ¼ **teaspoon ground black pepper**

Cucumber Salsa

- ½ **medium unpeeled cucumber, seeded and coarsely chopped (1 cup)**
- 2 **tablespoons coarsely chopped red onion**
- ⅓ **cup pitted ripe olives, sliced**
- ¼ **cup diced red bell pepper**

1. For chicken and marinade, rinse chicken and pat dry with paper towels. Trim any excess fat from chicken using **Kitchen Shears**. Zest lemons using **Lemon Zester/Scorer** to measure 1 tablespoon zest. Juice lemons using **Juicer** to measure ½ cup juice. Place zest and juice in **Small Batter Bowl**. Press garlic into batter bowl using **Garlic Press**. Add oil, oregano, paprika, salt and black pepper; whisk using **Mini-Whipper**. Remove 2 tablespoons of the marinade and reserve for use in the salsa.

2. Place chicken and remaining marinade in resealable plastic food storage bag; turn to coat. Marinate in refrigerator 2-4 hours, turning occasionally.

3. Meanwhile, for salsa, coarsely chop cucumber and onion using **Food Chopper**. Slice olives using **Egg Slicer Plus®**; dice bell pepper using **Chef's Knife**. Place vegetables in small bowl; add reserved 2 tablespoons marinade and mix gently. Cover and refrigerate until ready to serve.

4. Prepare grill for indirect cooking over medium coals. Remove chicken from marinade; discard plastic bag with marinade. Place chicken, skin side up, on grid of grill using **Barbecue Tongs**. Grill, covered, 45-50 minutes or until chicken registers 180°F in thickest part of thigh portion and juices run clear. Serve salsa with chicken.

Yield: 4 servings

Nutrients per serving: Calories 470, Total Fat 27 g, Saturated Fat 6 g, Cholesterol 150 mg, Carbohydrate 7 g, Protein 50 g, Sodium 520 mg, Fiber 2 g

Diabetic exchanges per serving: 1 vegetable, 6 meat

Italian-Style Grilled Pizza

Prep time: 30 minutes   Grill time: 12-15 minutes

Farmstand tomatoes, fresh basil leaves and mozzarella cheese create an Italian-style pizza that tastes like it has been baked in a traditional wood-fired oven.

1   **cup (4 ounces) shredded mozzarella cheese**

¼   **cup (1 ounce) grated fresh Parmesan cheese**

4   **plum tomatoes, seeded and diced (1½ cups)**

¼   **cup fresh basil leaves, sliced into fine ribbons**

1   **can (2.25 ounces) sliced pitted ripe olives, drained**

2   **tablespoons olive oil**

1   **tablespoon red wine vinegar**

2   **garlic cloves, pressed**

½   **teaspoon *each* salt and coarsely ground black pepper**

1   **package (16 ounces) prebaked pizza crust**

1. Prepare grill for direct cooking over medium coals. Place mozzarella cheese in **Classic Batter Bowl**. Grate Parmesan cheese into batter bowl using **Deluxe Cheese Grater**. Slice tomatoes in half using **Chef's Knife**; remove seeds using **Cook's Corer™**. Cut tomatoes into ¾-inch pieces; slice basil leaves into fine ribbons. Add tomatoes, basil and olives to batter bowl; mix gently using **Small Mix 'N Scraper®**.

2. In **Small Batter Bowl**, combine oil, vinegar, garlic pressed with **Garlic Press**, salt and black pepper. Lightly brush top of crust with 1 tablespoon of the oil mixture using **Pastry Brush**.

3. Place crust in center of grid of grill, top side down. Grill crust, uncovered, 4-5 minutes or until deep golden brown. Using **Barbecue Turner**, turn crust over and carefully remove to **Large Grooved Cutting Board**.

4. Add remaining oil mixture to cheese mixture in batter bowl; mix well. Spoon cheese mixture evenly over top of crust; return pizza to grid of grill. Cover and grill 8-10 minutes or until cheese is melted and bottom of crust is deep golden brown.

5. Remove pizza to cutting board; slice using **Pizza Cutter**. Place on **Round Platter**; serve using **Slice 'N Serve®**.

Yield: 4 servings

Nutrients per serving: Calories 500, Total Fat 21 g, Saturated Fat 6 g, Cholesterol 30 mg, Carbohydrate 55 g, Protein 26 g, Sodium 1290 mg, Fiber 3 g

Diabetic exchanges per serving: 3½ starch, 1 vegetable, 2 meat (3½ carb)

Cook's Tips

▲ To easily slice basil into ribbons, stack basil leaves on top of each other and roll lengthwise into a tight cylinder. Slice crosswise using chef's knife; separate into ribbons.

▲ For a heartier pizza, 1-2 cups grilled chicken or steak, cut into cubes, can be added to pizza toppings. Proceed as recipe directs.

▲ Substitute ¼ cup Italian salad dressing for the oil, vinegar, garlic, salt and black pepper in Step 2, if desired. Proceed as recipe directs.

MENU SUGGESTION

Serve with tossed mixed greens or *Strawberry Spinach Salad* (p. 40) and fruit sorbet for a light supper on the patio.

Grilled Rosemary Pork Chops

Prep time: 10 minutes   Grill time: 12-16 minutes

Serve these moist and tender pork chops with Hot German Potato Salad (p. 16). Let the potato salad get a head start cooking before adding the seasoned chops to the grill.

4 boneless pork loin chops, cut ³/₄-1 inch thick (about 6 ounces each)

4 teaspoons olive oil

2 teaspoons *Pantry Rosemary Herb Seasoning Mix*

1. Prepare grill for direct cooking over medium coals. Using **Pastry Brush**, brush both sides of pork chops with oil; sprinkle evenly with seasoning mix.

2. Place pork chops on grid of grill. Grill, covered, 12-16 minutes or until internal temperature reaches 160°F for well done, turning once using **Barbecue Tongs**.

Yield: 4 servings

Nutrients per serving: Calories 470, Total Fat 25 g, Saturated Fat 10 g, Cholesterol 175 mg, Carbohydrate 4 g, Protein 53 g, Sodium 410 mg, Fiber 0 g

Diabetic exchanges per serving: 1 vegetable, 6 meat

Cook's Tip

▲ These pork chops are also delicious when served with a quick mustard sauce. For *Dijon Mustard Sauce*, heat 1 cup half-and-half just to boiling in **Petite (1¹/₂-qt.) Saucepan**. Remove from heat. Whisk in 1 tablespoon Dijon mustard and 1 tablespoon snipped fresh parsley. Serve with pork chops.

MENU SUGGESTION

Serve steamed broccoli spears and marbled rye bread with butter alongside the pork chops and *Hot German Potato Salad* (p. 16).

▲ Be sure to scrub potatoes well to remove any dirt from the skins before you slice them.

▲ The Ultimate Slice & Grate perfectly cuts potatoes into very thin slices, eliminating the need to precook the potatoes for this side dish. To safely cut foods, always use the food holder when using the Ultimate Slice & Grate.

Hot German Potato Salad

Prep time: 20 minutes   Grill time: 30-35 minutes

This tangy, grilled potato dish is accented with bacon and onions, and perfectly complements the flavor of grilled pork chops or sausages.

1½ **cups water**
½ **cup cider vinegar**
¼ **cup sugar**
2 **tablespoons all-purpose flour**
1½ **teaspoons salt**
¼ **teaspoon ground black pepper**
1 **pound unpeeled red potatoes (3-4 medium)**
1 **medium onion, peeled and cut in half**
6 **slices bacon, crisply cooked and cut up**
2 **tablespoons snipped fresh parsley**
1 **heavy-duty foil pan (12 x 9 x 1½ inches)**

1. Prepare grill for direct cooking over medium coals. In large **Colander Bowl**, whisk together water, vinegar, sugar, flour, salt and black pepper using **Stainless Steel Whisk**.

2. Using **Ultimate Slice & Grate** fitted with v-shaped blade, slice potatoes and onion into vinegar mixture in bowl. Add bacon and parsley snipped with **Kitchen Shears**; mix gently with **Mix 'N Scraper®**. Spoon into foil pan. Cover with aluminum foil.

3. Place pan on grid of grill; cover grill. Grill 30-35 minutes or until potatoes are tender.

Yield: 4 servings

Nutrients per serving: Calories 340, Total Fat 14 g, Saturated Fat 5 g, Cholesterol 25 mg, Carbohydrate 41 g, Protein 12 g, Sodium 1340 mg, Fiber 2 g

Diabetic exchanges per serving: 2½ starch, ½ meat, 2½ fat (2½ carb)

Grilled Ratatouille

Prep and cook time: 30 minutes   Grill time: 10-12 minutes

Ratatouille (pronounced ra-tuh-TOO-ee) is a specialty vegetable dish from the Provence region of France. This version, featuring grilled vegetables, is delicious served hot or at room temperature.

Dressing

    2 **tablespoons balsamic vinegar**
    2 **garlic cloves, pressed**
    2 **teaspoons dried oregano leaves**
    ½ **teaspoon salt**

Vegetables and Pasta

    5 **plum tomatoes, cut in half lengthwise**
    1 **medium eggplant (1½ pounds), cut into ½-inch slices**
    1 **medium zucchini, cut into ½-inch slices**
    1 **large green bell pepper, seeded and cut into quarters**
    1 **large sweet onion, cut into ½-inch slices**
    ¼ **cup olive or vegetable oil**
    2 **tablespoons snipped fresh parsley**
    1 **pound uncooked penne or rigatoni pasta**
        Grated fresh Parmesan cheese (optional)

1. For dressing, combine vinegar, garlic pressed with **Garlic Press**, oregano and salt in **Small Batter Bowl**; whisk using **Stainless Steel Whisk** and set aside.

2. Prepare grill for direct cooking over medium coals. Using **Chef's Knife**, prepare vegetables. Brush vegetables with oil using **Pastry Brush**. Snip parsley using **Kitchen Shears** and set aside.

3. Meanwhile, bring 4 quarts water to a boil in **Professional (8-qt.) Stockpot**. Cook pasta according to package directions; drain and keep warm.

4. Place vegetables on grid of grill. Grill onion 10-12 minutes and tomatoes, eggplant, zucchini and bell pepper 6-8 minutes, uncovered, turning once with **Barbecue Tongs**.

5. Remove vegetables from grill; cut into bite-size pieces. Place vegetables in large **Colander Bowl**; drizzle with dressing and mix gently using **Mix 'N Scraper®**.

6. Place pasta in large shallow pasta bowl or platter. Spoon vegetable mixture over warm pasta. Sprinkle with parsley. Serve with Parmesan cheese, if desired.

Yield: 8 servings

Nutrients per serving: Calories 310, Total Fat 8 g, Saturated Fat 1.5 g, Cholesterol 0 g, Carbohydrate 53 g, Protein 10 g, Sodium 160 mg, Fiber 6 g

Diabetic exchanges per serving: 3 starch, 1 vegetable, 1 fat (3 carb)

Cook's Tips

▲ Hot cooked rice can be substituted for the pasta, if desired.

▲ This versatile vegetable mixture can be served as a side dish accompaniment or as an appetizer with toasted canapé bread slices or crackers. Simply omit the cooked pasta.

▲ Leftover grilled vegetables are great for adding flavor, variety and nutrition to everyday meals. Stir them into your favorite pasta sauce, top a pre-baked pizza crust or bread shell, or add to soups, stews and chili.

MENU SUGGESTION

A platter of assorted sliced cheeses and crusty *Grilled Garlic Bread* (p. 25) would perfectly complement the robust flavors of this grilled vegetable dish. Finish the meal in style with *Lemon Blueberry Cheesecake Torte* (p. 113).

Mediterranean Steak Salad

Prep time: 20 minutes   Marinate time: 6-8 hours or overnight   Grill time: 17-21 minutes

Making this hearty salad on a weeknight is a cinch. Just marinate the steak in the morning and finish preparation after work.

Marinade and Steak

- ⅔ cup **balsamic vinaigrette salad dressing**
- 4 **garlic cloves, pressed**
- 1½ teaspoons **dried oregano leaves**
- ⅛ teaspoon **coarsely ground black pepper**
- 1 **beef flank steak (1½-2 pounds)**

Salad

- 1 can (14 ounces) **artichoke hearts in water, drained and cut into quarters**
- 3 **plum tomatoes, cut into wedges**
- 1 cup **cucumber slices, cut in half**
- ½ small **red onion, sliced into thin wedges**
- ½ cup **pitted ripe olives, sliced**
- 1 bag (10 ounces) **hearts of romaine lettuce, torn into pieces (8 cups)**
- 1 package (4 ounces) **crumbled feta cheese**
- ¾ cup **balsamic vinaigrette salad dressing**

1. For marinade, combine dressing, garlic pressed with **Garlic Press**, oregano and black pepper in **Small Batter Bowl**; whisk using **Stainless Steel Whisk**. Place steak and marinade in resealable plastic food storage bag; turn to coat. Marinate in refrigerator 6-8 hours or overnight, turning occasionally.

2. Prepare grill for direct cooking over medium coals. For salad, quarter artichoke hearts and cut tomatoes into wedges using **Chef's Knife**. Slice cucumber using **Ultimate Slice & Grate**; cut slices in half. Slice onion into thin wedges. Slice olives with **Egg Slicer Plus®**.

3. Remove steak from marinade; discard marinade. Place steak on grid of grill. Grill, uncovered, 17-21 minutes or until steak is medium rare (145°F) to medium (160°F) doneness, turning occasionally using **Barbecue Tongs**. Remove steak from grill to **Large Grooved Cutting Board**. Carve steak diagonally across the grain into thin slices using **Carving Set** (see Cook's Tip).

4. Arrange lettuce on large serving platter; top with steak slices, artichokes, tomatoes, cucumber, onion and olives. Top with feta cheese. Serve salad using **3-Way Tongs**; drizzle with dressing.

Yield: 6 servings

Nutrients per serving: Calories 520, Total Fat 33 g, Saturated Fat 10 g, Cholesterol 85 mg, Carbohydrate 19 g, Protein 38 g, Sodium 880 mg, Fiber 6 g

Diabetic exchanges per serving: 1 starch, 5 meat, 1½ fat (1 carb)

MENU SUGGESTION

Accompany this main-dish salad with *Cheesy Pita Bread Wedges* (p. 25) and tall glasses of iced tea with fresh lemon. Serve a selection of bakery pastries for dessert.

Cajun Chicken Salad

Prep time: 30 minutes   Bake time: 10 minutes   Grill time: 12-15 minutes

Grilled chicken and toasted pecans get a Cajun kick in this lively main course salad.

Spiced Pecans

- ¾ **cup pecan halves**
- 2 **teaspoons vegetable oil**
- 1 **tablespoon sugar**
- 1½ **teaspoons *Pantry Cajun Herb Seasoning Mix***

Salad

- 1 **small yellow summer squash, scored, sliced and cut in half**
- 1 **small green bell pepper, seeded, cut into rings and quartered**
- 1 **cup cherry tomato halves**
- 1 **package (10 ounces) mixed salad greens with romaine and leaf lettuce**
- 4 **boneless, skinless chicken breast halves (4-6 ounces each)**
- 1 **tablespoon vegetable oil**
- 4 **teaspoons *Pantry Cajun Herb Seasoning Mix***
- ¾ **cup ranch salad dressing**
  Bountiful Bread Bowl (p. 24), optional

1. Preheat oven to 350°F. For spiced pecans, toss pecans with oil in **Small Batter Bowl**. Sprinkle with combined sugar and seasoning mix; toss until coated. Spread pecans in single layer over bottom of **Small Bar Pan**. Bake 10 minutes until lightly toasted. Remove from oven; cool pecans in bar pan.

2. Prepare grill for direct cooking over medium coals. Meanwhile, for salad, score summer squash lengthwise using **Lemon Zester/Scorer**. Slice squash using **Ultimate Slice & Grate** fitted with v-shaped blade; cut slices in half. Cut bell pepper into rings; cut rings into quarters. Cut cherry tomatoes in half. Toss vegetables with greens; refrigerate until ready to serve.

3. Rinse chicken; pat dry with paper towels. Brush with oil using **Pastry Brush**. Rub with seasoning mix. Place chicken on grid of grill. Grill, uncovered, 12-15 minutes or until chicken is no longer pink in the center, turning occasionally using **Barbecue Tongs**.

4. Remove chicken from grill. Cut chicken crosswise into slices on **Cutting Board** using **Carving Set**. Arrange chicken over salad in *Bountiful Bread Bowl* or on **Oval Platter**. Sprinkle with spiced pecans. Serve salad using **Large Serving Tongs**; drizzle with dressing.

Yield: 4 servings

Nutrients per serving: Calories 520, Total Fat 39 g, Saturated Fat 4.5 g, Cholesterol 85 mg, Carbohydrate 15 g, Protein 32 g, Sodium 570 mg, Fiber 5 g

Diabetic exchanges per serving: 1 starch, 4 meat, 3½ fat (1 carb)

Cook's Tips

▲ On hot summer days, conserve energy and keep your kitchen cool by using a toaster oven to prepare the spiced pecans. Bake at 350°F for 8 minutes. The **Small Bar Pan** is a convenient size for all your small-scale cooking in any toaster oven.

▲ The chicken can also be prepared using the **Professional Grill Pan**. Heat pan over medium-high heat 5 minutes. Prepare chicken as directed in Step 3. Place chicken in pan. Cook 5-7 minutes; turn using **Nylon Tongs**. Continue cooking 5-7 minutes or until chicken is no longer pink in the center.

MENU SUGGESTION

Once the salad is served, cut the bowl into wedges and enjoy this unique bread accompaniment. *Bananas Foster Stir-Fry* (p.121), our version of the New Orleans specialty, would make the perfect finish.

Cook's Tips

▲ The dough is easiest to handle when cold. Keep it refrigerated until you are ready to use it and work quickly when shaping the bread bowl.

▲ Gently insert the **Citrus Peeler** between the bread and baking bowl to loosen.

Bountiful Bread Bowl

Prep time: 10 minutes   Bake time: 15-18 minutes

For special occasions, our unique bread bowl
makes an impressive serving bowl for salad. (Pictured on p. 22)

1   **package (11 ounces) refrigerated French bread dough**

1. Preheat oven to 350°F. Generously spray outside of **Stoneware Baking Bowl** with nonstick cooking spray. Place baking bowl upside down on counter. Unroll bread dough onto flat side of **Large Grooved Cutting Board**.

2. Starting on one long side, gather up dough and quickly place over outside of baking bowl. (Do not press dough onto baking bowl.) Lightly pinch sides of dough together and trim off excess dough at corners with **Kitchen Shears**.

3. Bake 15-18 minutes or until deep golden brown. Remove from oven to **Stackable Cooling Rack**. Carefully loosen bread from baking bowl. Cool bread bowl on baking bowl 15 minutes. Carefully remove bread from baking bowl. Turn upright; cool 5 minutes.

Yield: 4 servings

Low Fat Nutrients per serving: Calories 190, Total Fat 2.5 g, Saturated Fat 1 g, Cholesterol 0 mg, Carbohydrate 34 g, Protein 6 g, Sodium 490 mg, Fiber 1 g

Diabetic exchanges per serving: 2½ starch (2½ carb)

Cheesy Pita Bread Wedges

Prep time: 10 minutes   Grill time: 3-4 minutes

These easy pita wedges would make a delicious bread accompaniment or hot appetizer. (Pictured on p. 21)

6   **pita pocket bread rounds, cut in half**

12 **tablespoons garlic and herb cream cheese spread**

3   **tablespoons olive oil**

¼   **teaspoon salt**

⅛   **teaspoon coarsely ground black pepper**

1. Prepare grill for direct cooking over medium coals. Cut pita bread rounds in half. Using **Small Spreader**, spread 1 tablespoon cheese in each pita half.

2. Combine oil, salt and black pepper. Brush both sides of each bread half with oil mixture using **Pastry Brush**.

3. Place bread halves on grid of grill. Grill, uncovered, 1½-2 minutes on each side or until lightly browned, turning with **Barbecue Tongs**. Cut bread halves into wedges.

Yield: 12 servings

Nutrients per serving: Calories 150, Total Fat 7 g, Saturated Fat .5 g, Cholesterol 10 mg, Carbohydrate 18 g, Protein 4 g, Sodium 280 mg, Fiber less than 1 g

Diabetic exchanges per serving: 1 starch, 1 fat (1 carb)

Cook's Tip

▲ The pita bread wedges can be made without the cream cheese spread, if desired.

Grilled Garlic Bread

Prep time: 5 minutes   Grill time: 3-4 minutes

Turn simple into sensational with a savory grilled side that goes with just about any summertime meal. (Pictured on p. 18)

1   **loaf (1 pound) Italian bread**

⅓   **cup butter or margarine, melted**

4   **garlic cloves, pressed**

1½ **teaspoons *Pantry Rosemary Herb Seasoning Mix* (optional)**

1. Prepare grill for direct cooking over medium to medium-low coals. Using **Serrated Bread Knife**, cut bread in half lengthwise.

2. Microwave butter in **Small Micro-Cooker®** on HIGH 45 seconds or until melted. Press garlic into butter using **Garlic Press**. Using **Pastry Brush**, brush butter mixture generously over cut surfaces of bread; sprinkle with seasoning mix, if desired. Cut each half into six 2-inch slices.

3. Place bread slices, buttered side down, on grid of grill. Grill, uncovered, 1½-2 minutes on each side or until toasted, turning with **Barbecue Tongs**.

Yield: 12 servings

Nutrients per serving (1 bread slice): Calories 150, Total Fat 6 g, Saturated Fat 3.5 g, Cholesterol 15 mg, Carbohydrate 20 g, Protein 3 g, Sodium 320 mg, Fiber 1 g

Diabetic exchanges per serving (1 bread slice): 1 starch, 1 fat (1 carb)

Cook's Tips

▲ If you prefer, substitute 1 tablespoon snipped fresh parsley for the seasoning mix.

▲ To bake the garlic bread, wrap bread in aluminum foil and bake at 375°F for 15 minutes or until hot.

Grilled Asparagus & Portobello Mushroom Salad

Prep time: 15 minutes   Grill time: 6-8 minutes

The flavors of fresh grilled vegetables come to life in this salad.

▲ The vinaigrette can be prepared ahead and refrigerated until ready to use. Mix well before using.

▲ Portobello mushrooms are flavorful, large, dark brown mushrooms with a dense meaty texture. They are particularly popular for grilling. They are available fresh, either packaged or in bulk, in the produce section of most supermarkets.

▲ Mushrooms should not be cleaned until ready to use. To remove dirt, wipe mushrooms with a damp paper towel or soft brush, or quickly rinse under cold running water and immediately pat dry.

▲ To trim asparagus, snap off and discard tough stem ends.

Vinaigrette

- ¼ **cup olive oil**
- 2 **tablespoons white wine vinegar**
- 1 **tablespoon Dijon mustard**
- 1 **teaspoon sugar**
- ⅛ **teaspoon** *each* **salt and coarsely ground black pepper**

Salad

- 1 **package (6 ounces) fresh portobello mushrooms, stems trimmed (3-4 large)**
- 1 **medium red bell pepper**
- 8 **ounces asparagus spears, trimmed**
- 1 **bag (5 ounces) spring mix salad blend of baby greens**
- 1 **ounce shaved fresh Parmesan cheese**

1. Prepare grill for direct cooking over medium coals. For vinaigrette, combine oil, vinegar, mustard, sugar, salt and black pepper in Measure, Mix, & Pour™; mix until well blended.

2. For salad, clean mushrooms. Cut bell pepper into quarters; remove membranes and seeds. Using Pastry Brush, brush mushroom caps, bell pepper quarters and asparagus with 3 tablespoons of the vinaigrette. Place vegetables on grid of grill positioning asparagus spears crosswise on grid. Grill vegetables, uncovered, 6-8 minutes or until crisp-tender, turning asparagus frequently and mushrooms and bell peppers once halfway through grilling using Barbecue Tongs.

3. Using Hold 'N Slice™ and Chef's Knife, slice mushrooms and bell peppers crosswise into ¼-inch-thick slices. Cut asparagus into 2-inch pieces. Toss vegetables with salad greens and remaining vinaigrette in large bowl; arrange on Oval Platter. Top with Parmesan cheese shaved with Cheese Knife. Serve using Large Serving Tongs.

Yield: 4 servings

Nutrients per serving: Calories 210, Total Fat 16 g, Saturated Fat 3 g, Cholesterol 5 mg, Carbohydrate 11 g, Protein 7 g, Sodium 315 mg, Fiber 4 g

Diabetic exchanges per serving: ½ starch, 1 meat, 2 fat (½ carb)

Mexican Burger Bar

Prep time: 45 minutes   Grill time: 11-13 minutes

With four distinctive flavor variations, this international burger is a must-have in your repertoire.

Burgers

- 2 **pounds (80% lean) ground beef**
- ¼ **cup finely chopped onion**
- 1 **tablespoon Worcestershire sauce**
- ½ **teaspoon salt**
- ¼ **teaspoon ground black pepper**
- 8 **slices (1 ounce each) Colby & Monterey Jack cheese blend**
- 8 **Kaiser rolls or hamburger buns, split**

Mexican Sandwich Spread

- ¼ **cup mayonnaise**
- ¼ **cup sour cream**
- 1½ **teaspoons *Pantry Southwestern Seasoning Mix***

Mexican Toppers

- 2 **medium tomatoes, sliced**
- 1 **large avocado, peeled and sliced**
- 1 **cup pickled jalapeño pepper slices, drained**

1. For burgers, crumble ground beef into **Classic Batter Bowl**. Finely chop onion using **Food Chopper**. Add onion, Worcestershire sauce, salt and black pepper to ground beef; mix gently but thoroughly. Form mixture into 8 round patties, ½ inch thick. Refrigerate, covered, until ready to grill.

2. For Mexican sandwich spread, combine mayonnaise, sour cream and seasoning mix in **Small Batter Bowl**; mix until well blended. Cover and refrigerate.

3. For Mexican toppers, slice tomatoes using **Ultimate Slice & Grate**. Slice avocado using **Chef's Knife**. Place toppers in individual serving bowls; cover and refrigerate.

4. When ready to grill, prepare grill for direct cooking over medium coals. Place patties on grid of grill. Grill, uncovered, 11-13 minutes or until centers are no longer pink, turning once using **Barbecue Turner**. About 1 minute before burgers are done, place cheese slices on top.

5. Meanwhile, place roll halves, cut side down, on grid of grill. Grill 1-2 minutes or until rolls are lightly toasted. Place burgers in rolls. Serve with spread and toppers.

Yield: 8 sandwiches

Nutrients per serving (1 burger, 1 roll, 1 tablespoon spread): Calories 680, Total Fat 40 g, Saturated Fat 17 g, Cholesterol 115 mg, Carbohydrate 45 g, Protein 35 g, Sodium 1370 mg, Fiber 5 g

Diabetic exchanges per serving (1 burger, 1 roll, 1 tablespoon spread): 2½ starch, 4 meat, 3½ fat (2½ carb)

Variations: *American Burger Bar:* Top burgers with American cheese slices. Use **Pantry Barbecue Seasoning Mix** in the sandwich spread. Serve with toppers such as leaf lettuce, tomato slices, dill pickle slices, sweet pickle relish, red onion rings or corn relish.

Italian Burger Bar: Top burgers with mozzarella or provolone cheese slices. Use **Pantry Italian Seasoning Mix** in the sandwich spread. Serve with toppers such as tomato slices, green bell pepper rings, mushroom slices, pitted ripe olive slices or giardiniera relish.

Greek Burger Bar: Omit cheese slices. Substitute pita bread pockets for rolls. Use **Pantry Lemon Pepper Seasoning Mix** in the sandwich spread. Serve with toppers such as crumbled feta cheese, fresh spinach leaves, tomato slices, red onion rings, cucumber slices or pitted ripe olive slices.

Cook's Tips

▲ Ground beef patties should be cooked to a minimum internal temperature of 160°F (medium doneness). The instant-read **Pocket Thermometer** is a helpful tool in determining meat doneness. Insert the thermometer into the side of the burgers about 2 inches to get an accurate temperature reading.

▲ For juicy burgers, avoid pressing or flattening ground beef patties with barbecue turner while grilling.

▲ Wear plastic gloves when working with fresh jalapeño peppers. Their seeds and membranes contain oils that will irritate your skin. Use the **Quikut Paring Knife** to cut peppers in half, then remove seeds and membranes using the **Cook's Corer**™.

▲ Be sure to drain the canned beans using the large **Colander**, then place the colander under cold running water to rinse beans.

Southwestern Two-Bean Salad

Prep time: 30 minutes   Chill time: 2-3 hours

*Pinto and black beans are a flavorful duo in a
new version of a marinated bean salad. (Pictured on p. 28)*

Dressing

    ½ **cup white vinegar**
    ¼ **cup vegetable oil**
    1 **tablespoon sugar**
    2 **teaspoons ground cumin**
    1 **teaspoon dried oregano leaves**
    ½ **teaspoon salt**
    ¼ **teaspoon ground black pepper**

Salad

    2 **cans (15 ounces each) pinto beans, drained and rinsed**
    1 **can (15 ounces) black beans, drained and rinsed**
    1 **can (15¼ ounces) whole kernel corn, drained**
    1 **large red bell pepper, chopped**
    ½ **cup finely chopped red onion**
    2 **fresh jalapeño peppers, seeded and finely chopped (¼-⅓ cup)**
    ¼ **cup snipped fresh cilantro**

1. For dressing, whisk together vinegar, oil, sugar, cumin, oregano, salt and black pepper in **Small Batter Bowl** using **Stainless Steel Whisk**; set aside.

2. For salad, drain and rinse beans using large **Colander**. Place beans in large **Colander Bowl**. Drain corn. Chop bell pepper using **Chef's Knife**; add corn and bell pepper to beans.

3. Chop onion and jalapeño peppers using **Food Chopper** (see Cook's Tip). Snip cilantro using **Kitchen Shears**. Add onion, jalapeño peppers, cilantro and dressing to bean mixture. Mix gently. Cover and refrigerate 2-3 hours to allow flavors to blend.

Yield: 12 servings

Nutrients per serving (½ cup): Calories 120, Total Fat 5 g, Saturated Fat 0 g, Cholesterol 0 mg, Carbohydrate 16 g, Protein 4 g, Sodium 370 mg, Fiber 4 g

Diabetic exchanges per serving: 1 starch, 1 fat (1 carb)

Creamy Potato Salad

Prep time: 15 minutes   Cook time: 14-16 minutes   Chill time: 2 hours

We know you'll like this picnic classic made with garden-fresh sugar snap peas, radish slices and green onions. (Pictured on p. 32)

3   **pounds unpeeled red potatoes, cut into 1-inch cubes (about 8 cups)**

8   **ounces sugar snap peas, cut in half (2 cups)**

1   **cup sliced radishes**

¼   **cup thinly sliced green onions with tops**

½   **cup mayonnaise**

½   **cup sour cream**

2   **tablespoons Dijon mustard**

1   **teaspoon salt**

¼   **teaspoon coarsely ground black pepper**

1. Bring 6 cups water to a boil in covered **Professional (8-qt.) Stockpot**. Cut potatoes into 1-inch cubes using **Chef's Knife**. Place in an even layer over bottom of **Steamer Insert** and position over boiling water. Cover; reduce heat so water continues to actively boil. Cook 14-16 minutes or just until potatoes are tender. Add snap peas during last 2 minutes of cooking time. Carefully remove steamer insert from stockpot. Cool potatoes and snap peas quickly by placing under cold running water.

2. Using **Ultimate Slice & Grate** fitted with adjustable blade, slice radishes. Thinly slice green onions with chef's knife.

3. Combine mayonnaise, sour cream, mustard, salt and black pepper in large **Colander Bowl**; mix until well blended. Add potatoes, snap peas, radishes and green onions; mix gently with **Mix 'N Scraper®**. Cover; refrigerate at least 2 hours or overnight.

Yield: 12 servings

Nutrients per serving (¾ cup): Calories 190, Total Fat 9 g, Saturated Fat 2.5 g, Cholesterol 15 mg, Carbohydrate 23 g, Protein 3 g, Sodium 320 mg, Fiber 2 g

Diabetic exchanges per serving: 1½ starch, 1½ fat (1½ carb)

Cook's Tips

▲ A sugar snap pea is an entirely edible–pod and all–sweet pea that is a cross between the English pea and the snow pea. They should be cooked only briefly to retain their crisp texture. They can also be eaten raw. They are found packaged in the produce section of most supermarkets.

▲ Substitute 1 cup frozen peas for the snap peas, if desired.

▲ This potato salad can be prepared up to 1 day in advance.

Barbecued Country-Style Pork Ribs

Prep time: 5 minutes   Cook time: 45 minutes to 1 hour, 15 minutes   Grill time: 10-12 minutes

A platter of tender, meaty pork ribs, glazed with your choice of homemade tomatoey barbecue sauce, is the signature of an American culinary classic.

4-5 **pounds country-style pork loin ribs**
  6 **cups water**
  2 **cans (14½ ounces each) beef broth**
  2 **bay leaves**
  2 **garlic cloves, pressed**
1½ **cups Blue Ribbon Barbecue Sauce, any flavor (p. 51)**

1. Place ribs in **Professional (8-qt.) Stockpot**. Add water, broth, bay leaves and garlic pressed with **Garlic Press**. Cover; bring to a boil. Reduce heat and simmer 45 minutes to 1 hour, 15 minutes or until pork is tender. Remove ribs from stockpot with **Nylon Tongs**.

2. Meanwhile, prepare grill for direct cooking over medium coals. Place ribs on grid of grill. Brush with barbecue sauce using **Barbecue Basting Brush**. Grill, uncovered, 10-12 minutes or until well glazed, brushing and turning frequently with **Barbecue Tongs**. Serve with additional heated barbecue sauce, if desired.

Yield: 8 servings

Nutrients per serving: Calories 300, Total Fat 14 g, Saturated Fat 5 g, Cholesterol 90 mg, Carbohydrate 16 g, Protein 27 g, Sodium 460 mg, Fiber 0 g

Diabetic exchanges per serving: 1 starch, 3 meat (1 carb)

Cook's Tips

▲ To make this recipe ahead, cook ribs up to 2 days before grilling. Wrap tightly and refrigerate until ready to grill.

▲ Country-style ribs may come bone-in or boneless. Both types can be used in this recipe. They are cut from the pork loin and are meatier than spareribs or back ribs.

▲ When basting grilled foods with barbecue sauce, baste the last 10-15 minutes of grilling to avoid burning.

MENU SUGGESTION

For a summer supper with all-family appeal, serve these meaty ribs with *Creamy Potato Salad* (p. 31) and *Corn on the Cob with Herb Butters* (p. 7). Light and refreshing *Dreamy Creamy Orange Pie* (p. 114) will keep the smiles coming.

Cook's Tips

▲ For an attractive presentation, thread scored lemon and lime wedges onto the ends of each skewer. The flavor of the grilled fruit wedges nicely complements the shrimp.

▲ Do not marinate the shrimp for more than 1 hour or the texture will become soft and mushy.

▲ To easily peel and devein the shrimp, insert the split blade of the **Grapefruit Knife** on either side of the shell on the back of the shrimp. With a rocking motion, cut and split the shell up to the tail to easily peel off the shell, leaving tail intact. With pointed end of the split blade, lift out vein. Rinse shrimp under cold running water.

▲ This recipe can be easily doubled.

Citrus Shrimp Skewers

Prep time: 20 minutes   Marinate time: 45 minutes to 1 hour   Grill time: 5-6 minutes

Marinating shrimp with citrus juices and orange marmalade gives these skewers a fresh flavor boost.

12	**ounces uncooked shell-on medium shrimp (about 30-40)**
2	**lemons**
2	**limes**
1/2	**cup orange marmalade**
1	**tablespoon vegetable oil**
1	**large garlic clove, pressed**
1	**tablespoon snipped fresh parsley**
1/4	**teaspoon ground red pepper**

1. Peel and devein shrimp, leaving tails on. Thread shrimp onto four 12-inch skewers; place in large resealable plastic food storage bag.

2. Using **Juicer**, juice lemons to measure 1/4 cup juice; juice limes to measure 1/4 cup juice. Pour juices into **Small Batter Bowl**. Add orange marmalade and oil. Using **Garlic Press**, press garlic into batter bowl. Snip parsley using **Kitchen Shears**. Add parsley and red pepper to ingredients in batter bowl; whisk using **Stainless Steel Whisk** until blended. Reserve 1/4 cup of the marinade for basting. Pour remaining marinade over shrimp. Marinate in refrigerator 45 minutes to 1 hour, turning occasionally.

3. Prepare grill for direct cooking over medium coals. Remove skewers from marinade; discard plastic bag with marinade. Place skewers on grid of grill; brush with reserved marinade using **Barbecue Basting Brush**. Grill, uncovered, 5-6 minutes or until shrimp appear opaque, turning once with **Barbecue Tongs** and brushing again with marinade.

Yield: 4 servings

Nutrients per serving: Calories 230, Total Fat 5 g, Saturated Fat 0 g, Cholesterol 130 mg, Carbohydrate 30 g, Protein 18 g, Sodium 150 mg, Fiber 0 g

Diabetic exchanges per serving: 2 starch, 1 meat (2 carb)

MENU SUGGESTION

Serve with *Calico Coleslaw* (p. 36) and grilled tomatoes (p. 49). The tomatoes can also be brushed with part of the reserved marinade during grilling for added flavor.

30 *Minutes or less*

Cook's Tips

▲ The dressing and the vegetables for this slaw can be prepared and refrigerated separately up to several hours in advance. To prevent the colorful vegetables from bleeding, do not add the dressing until just before you are ready to serve the salad.

▲ To remove the core from a whole head of cabbage, cut cabbage in half. Using Chef's Knife, carefully cut on either side of the core making a v-shaped wedge cut. Remove the core.

Calico Coleslaw

Prep time: 25 minutes

This colorful, vibrant and refreshing slaw will make any picnic plate a standout. (Pictured on p. 35)

Dressing

 1 orange
 1/4 cup rice vinegar
 1 1/2 tablespoons vegetable oil
 2 tablespoons honey
 2 tablespoons snipped fresh cilantro
 1/2 teaspoon salt

Slaw

 1/2 head red cabbage, cored and shredded (2 cups)
 2 large carrots, cut into julienne strips (1 cup)
 1 small red bell pepper, seeded and cut into thin strips (1 cup)
 1 small yellow bell pepper, seeded and cut into thin strips (1 cup)
 2 green onions, tops only, cut into thin strips (1/2 cup)

1. For dressing, zest orange using **Lemon Zester/Scorer** to measure 1 teaspoon zest. Juice orange with **Juicer** to measure 2 tablespoons juice. Place zest, juice, vinegar, oil, honey, cilantro and salt in **Measure, Mix, & Pour**™. Mix thoroughly and set aside.

2. For slaw, cut cabbage half into 2 equal portions. Using **Ultimate Slice & Grate** fitted with v-shaped blade, carefully slice cabbage into thin shreds. Peel carrots and cut into julienne strips using **Julienne Peeler**. Cut bell peppers into thin strips using **Chef's Knife**. Cut off white parts of green onions and reserve for another use. Slice green onion tops into thin, short strips. Place vegetables in large **Colander Bowl**.

3. When ready to serve, pour dressing over slaw; toss using **3-Way Tongs**. Serve immediately.

Yield: 8 servings

Low Fat Nutrients per serving (3/4 cup): Calories 60, Total Fat 3 g, Saturated Fat 0 g, Cholesterol 0 mg, Carbohydrate 9 g, Protein less than 1 g, Sodium 150 mg, Fiber 1 g

Diabetic exchanges per serving (3/4 cup): 1 starch (1 carb)

Minted Melon Medley

Prep time: 15 minutes   Stand time: 30 minutes

You'll find this refreshing melon combination equally nice for a side dish or dessert. (Pictured on cover)

Syrup

- **6 fresh mint leaves**
- **⅓ cup water**
- **3 tablespoons sugar**

Fruit

- **3 cups honeydew melon cubes**
- **3 cups seedless watermelon balls**
- **2 cups cantaloupe balls**
- **½ cup blueberries**
- **Additional mint leaves, snipped (optional)**

1. Snip mint leaves in half using **Kitchen Shears**. In **Petite (1½-qt.) Saucepan**, combine mint leaves, water and sugar. Heat over low heat, stirring with **Bamboo Spoon** until sugar is dissolved. Bring to a simmer; let simmer 6-8 minutes. Remove from heat; cool to room temperature, about 30 minutes.

2. Meanwhile, for fruit, cut honeydew melon into cubes using **Crinkle Cutter**. Scoop watermelon and cantaloupe into balls using **Small Scoop**.

3. Place fruit in serving bowl; pour cooled syrup over fruit. Toss gently using **3-Way Tongs**. Serve immediately or refrigerate up to 1 hour. Garnish with additional mint leaves snipped with kitchen shears, if desired.

Yield: 8 servings

Low Fat Nutrients per serving (1 cup): Calories 80, Total Fat 0 g, Saturated Fat 0 g, Cholesterol 0 mg, Carbohydrate 20 g, Protein 1 g, Sodium 10 mg, Fiber 1 g

Diabetic exchanges per serving (1 cup): 1 starch (1 carb)

Variation: *Minted Fruit Medley* (Pictured on p. 38): Substitute 6 cups sliced nectarines and ½ pint fresh raspberries for the melons. Proceed as recipe directs.

Cook's Tips

▲ This recipe can be easily doubled for larger crowds.

▲ You will need about ½ of a medium honeydew melon, 1 cantaloupe and ½ of a small seedless watermelon to make this recipe.

Bistro Turkey Burgers

Prep time: 20 minutes   Grill time: 12-14 minutes

Topped with smoky grilled onions and Swiss cheese, these are no ordinary burgers.

- **1 envelope (1 ounce) dry onion soup mix, divided**
- **¼ cup plus 2 tablespoons water**
- **1 pound lean (93%) ground turkey**
- **1 egg white**
- **2 tablespoons snipped fresh parsley**
- **1 garlic clove, pressed**
- **4 red or sweet yellow onion slices, cut ½ inch thick**
- **4 slices (1 ounce each) Swiss cheese**
- **4 onion rolls, split**
- **4 tablespoons honey mustard**

1. Prepare grill for direct cooking over medium coals. In **Classic Batter Bowl**, combine 3 tablespoons of the soup mix with 2 tablespoons of the water. Add turkey, egg white, parsley snipped with **Kitchen Shears** and garlic pressed with **Garlic Press**; mix lightly but thoroughly using **Pastry Blender**. Form turkey mixture into 4 round patties, ½ inch thick.

2. For basting sauce, combine remaining 1 tablespoon soup mix with ¼ cup water in **Small Micro-Cooker®**. Microwave on HIGH 30 seconds.

3. Place patties and onion slices on grid of grill. Brush both with basting sauce using **Barbecue Basting Brush**. Grill, uncovered, 5 minutes; turn patties and onions with **Barbecue Turner** and brush with basting sauce. Grill 5-6 minutes or until meat is no longer pink in center and onion is tender. Place 1 slice of cheese on each patty; grill an additional minute or until cheese is melted. Remove from grill.

4. Meanwhile, place roll halves, cut side down, on grid of grill. Grill 1-2 minutes or until rolls are lightly toasted. Place burgers on bottom halves of rolls. Spread 1 tablespoon mustard on top half of roll and top with onion slice.

Yield: 4 sandwiches

Nutrients per serving: Calories 520, Total Fat 25 g, Saturated Fat 11 g, Cholesterol 120 mg, Carbohydrate 41 g, Protein 35 g, Sodium 1120 mg, Fiber 3 g

Diabetic exchanges per serving: 2½ starch, 4 meat (2½ carb)

Cook's Tips

▲ Use the **Egg Separator** to easily separate egg white from yolk. Refrigerate the leftover yolk and add it to scrambled eggs or French toast batter for tomorrow's breakfast.

▲ A bistro is a small café or pub, usually serving modest, down-to-earth food. The word originates from the French word *bistrot*, meaning "pub."

▲ You can prepare and shape these burgers in advance. Wrap tightly in plastic wrap and refrigerate up to 1 day before grilling.

MENU SUGGESTION

Minted Fruit Medley (p. 37) makes a refreshing accompaniment to these hearty burgers.

30 *Minutes or less*

Cook's Tips

▲ The thin brown skin on sliced natural almonds makes these nuts an attractive choice in this salad. Oven toasting gives them extra crunch and flavor.

▲ Always toss salad greens with the dressing just before serving to avoid soggy, limp salads.

Strawberry Spinach Salad

Prep time: 20 minutes   Bake time: 10-12 minutes

Strawberries, toasted almonds and a tangy dressing make this refreshing salad simply unforgettable.

Dressing
- 1 **lemon**
- 2 **tablespoons white wine vinegar**
- 1/3 **cup sugar**
- 1 **tablespoon vegetable oil**
- 1 **teaspoon poppy seeds**

Salad
- 1/4 **cup sliced natural almonds, toasted**
- 8 **ounces (1 1/2 cups) strawberries, hulled and quartered**
- 1/2 **medium cucumber, sliced and cut in half**
- 1/4 **small red onion, sliced into thin wedges (1/4 cup)**
- 1 **package (6 ounces) baby spinach**

1. For dressing, zest lemon using **Lemon Zester/Scorer** to measure 1/2 teaspoon zest. Juice lemon using **Juicer** to measure 2 tablespoons juice. Combine zest, juice, vinegar, sugar, oil and poppy seeds in **Small Batter Bowl**. Whisk until well blended using **Mini-Whipper**. Cover; refrigerate until ready to use.

2. Preheat oven to 350°F. For salad, spread almonds in single layer over bottom of **Small Bar Pan**. Bake 10-12 minutes or until lightly toasted. Remove from oven; cool almonds in bar pan.

3. Meanwhile, hull strawberries using **Cook's Corer™**; cut strawberries into quarters.

4. Score cucumber lengthwise using lemon zester/scorer; remove seeds using **The Corer™**. Using **Ultimate Slice & Grate** fitted with v-shaped blade, slice cucumber; cut slices in half. Slice onion into thin wedges.

5. Place spinach in large serving bowl; add strawberries, cucumber and onion. Whisk dressing; pour over salad, gently tossing to coat using **3-Way Tongs**. Sprinkle with almonds. Serve immediately.

Yield: 10 servings

Low Fat Nutrients per serving (1 cup): Calories 70, Total Fat 3 g, Saturated Fat 0 g, Cholesterol 0 mg, Carbohydrate 10 g, Protein 1 g, Sodium 15 mg, Fiber 1 g

Diabetic exchanges per serving (1 cup): 1/2 starch, 1/2 fat (1/2 carb)

Picnic Sausage & Potato Kebabs

Prep time: 35 minutes   Microwave time: 5-7 minutes   Grill time: 6-8 minutes

You've seen bratwurst on the grill before, but never quite like this!

Mustard Sauce

- ¼ **cup mayonnaise**
- 2 **tablespoons stone-ground mustard**

Kebabs

- ¾ **pound petite new potatoes (10-12)**
- ¼ **cup water**
- 1 **teaspoon olive oil**
- 1 **garlic clove, pressed**
- ¾ **teaspoon dried dill weed**
- ⅛ **teaspoon *each* salt and ground black pepper**
- 6 **large green onions**
- 1 **package (1 pound) cooked bratwurst (5-6 sausages)**
- 12 **cherry tomatoes**

1. Prepare grill for direct cooking over medium coals. For mustard sauce, mix mayonnaise and mustard in small bowl. Cover and refrigerate until ready to serve.

2. For kebabs, cut potatoes in half using **Crinkle Cutter**. Place potatoes and water in **Large Micro-Cooker®**; cover. Microwave on HIGH 5-7 minutes, just until potatoes are fork-tender; drain. Drizzle with oil. Add garlic pressed with **Garlic Press** and seasonings; mix gently using **Small Mix 'N Scraper®**.

3. Trim root ends from green onions. Cut 24 pieces, each 2 inches long. Reserve green tops for another use. Add onions to potatoes and toss gently.

4. Cut bratwurst diagonally into 1-inch pieces. Alternately thread bratwurst, potatoes, onions and cherry tomatoes onto six 12-inch skewers.

5. Grill kebabs, uncovered, 6-8 minutes or until bratwurst is browned, turning frequently using **Barbecue Tongs**. Serve kebabs with mustard sauce.

Yield: 6 servings

Nutrients per serving: Calories 370, Total Fat 28 g, Saturated Fat 9 g, Cholesterol 52 mg, Carbohydrate 16 g, Protein 13 g, Sodium 610 mg, Fiber 2 g

Diabetic exchanges per serving: 1 starch, 1½ meat, 4 fat (1 carb)

Cook's Tips

▲ For extra convenience, this recipe calls for precooked bratwurst. If you prefer to use fresh bratwurst, you'll need to cook the sausages before skewering. To cook fresh bratwurst before grilling, prick sausages several times. Place in **Large (10-in.) Skillet** with 3 cups water and 1 medium onion, cut into wedges. Bring to a boil. Reduce heat; cover and simmer 10 minutes. Remove bratwurst from skillet using **Nylon Tongs**; cool slightly and proceed as recipe directs.

▲ Precooked smoked sausage is another type of sausage that can be used in this recipe.

▲ If you use wooden skewers, be sure to soak them in water for at least 30 minutes before using to prevent burning.

MENU SUGGESTION

Serve with sauerkraut or marinated cucumber salad and rye or pumpernickel rolls. Enjoy *Apple Berry Crisp* (p. 118) for dessert.

▲ It's easy to drain and rinse the 2 cans of kidney beans at one time in the large **Colander**.

▲ A big advantage to using Stoneware is that it retains heat after baking. These zesty beans will stay warm in our Stoneware Baking Bowl for a long time.

Tangy Barbecue Beans

Prep time: 20 minutes   Bake time: 30 minutes

No backyard barbecue is complete without this simple, well-seasoned side dish that's guaranteed to stay warm and satisfying throughout the party.

½	**pound sliced bacon**
1	**cup chopped onion**
3	**garlic cloves, pressed**
½	**cup packed brown sugar**
2	**tablespoons cider or white vinegar**
½	**cup ketchup**
2	**teaspoons Tabasco® pepper sauce (optional)**
4	**cans (15-16 ounces each) pork and beans in tomato sauce, undrained**
2	**cans (15.5 ounces each) dark red kidney beans, drained and rinsed**

1. Preheat oven to 375°F. Cook bacon in **Family (12-in.) Skillet** over medium heat until crisp. Remove bacon to paper towels. Reserve 2 tablespoons drippings in skillet. Break cooked bacon into large crumbles; set aside. Cook onion in drippings over medium heat 3-4 minutes or until crisp-tender, stirring occasionally. Press garlic into skillet using **Garlic Press**, cook and stir 1 minute.

2. Add brown sugar and vinegar to skillet; cook and stir until sugar is dissolved and mixture is bubbly. Add bacon, ketchup, pepper sauce and beans to skillet. Bring mixture to a boil; remove skillet from heat. Carefully spoon bean mixture into **Stoneware Baking Bowl** using **Nylon Spoon**.

3. Bake 30 minutes or until bubbly and heated through.

Yield: 16-18 servings

Nutrients per serving (½ cup): Calories 210, Total Fat 6 g, Saturated Fat 2 g, Cholesterol 15 mg, Carbohydrate 35 g, Protein 8 g, Sodium 590 mg, Fiber 6 g

Diabetic exchanges per serving (½ cup): 2 starch, 1 fat (2 carb)

MENU SUGGESTION

Tangy Barbecue Beans and *Family Pasta Salad* (p. 46) are tasty side dishes to serve next to your favorite grilled hot dogs or hamburgers.

▲ This pasta salad can
be prepared up to 1 day
in advance. For a
creamier salad, simply
add additional
mayonnaise and/or
yogurt before serving.

▲ You can substitute
any 2-inch tube-shaped
pasta or elbow spring
macaroni for the pasta
in this salad.

Family Pasta Salad

Prep and cook time: 30 minutes   Chill time: 2 hours

*The entire family will delight in this colorful pasta salad. Spiral-shaped
noodles add a fun "twist" to a classic favorite.* (Pictured on p. 45)

1 **package (16 ounces) uncooked
cavatappi pasta**
1 **package (8 ounces) mild cheddar
cheese, cut into 1/2-inch cubes**
1 **cup frozen peas, thawed**
1/2 **cup sliced celery**
1/4 **cup finely chopped onion**
1 **small carrot, grated**
1 **cup light mayonnaise**
1 **container (8 ounces) plain
fat-free yogurt**
1/2 **teaspoon salt**
1/8 **teaspoon ground black pepper**

1. Cook pasta according to package directions in
Professional (8-qt.) Stockpot; drain using large
Colander.

2. Meanwhile, cut cheese into 1/2-inch cubes
using **Crinkle Cutter**.

3. Place frozen peas in small **Colander** and rinse
under cold running water to thaw; drain. Slice
celery using **Chef's Knife**. Finely chop onion
using **Food Chopper**. Grate carrot using
Deluxe Cheese Grater fitted with coarse
grating drum.

4. Place pasta in large **Colander Bowl**. Add
cheese cubes, peas, celery, onion and carrot;
mix gently using **Mix 'N Scraper®**.

5. Combine mayonnaise, yogurt, salt and black
pepper in **Small Batter Bowl**; stir into pasta
mixture. Cover; refrigerate at least 2 hours
before serving.

Yield: 16 servings

Nutrients per serving (1 cup): Calories 220, Total Fat 10 g,
Saturated Fat 4 g, Cholesterol 20 mg, Carbohydrate 24 g,
Protein 8 g, Sodium 310 mg, Fiber 2 g

Diabetic exchanges per serving: 1 1/2 starch, 1/2 meat, 1 fat
(1 1/2 carb)

Grilled Onion Flowers

Prep time: 10 minutes   Microwave time: 6 minutes   Grill time: 15 minutes

These unusual blossoms are the perfect accompaniment to grilled steak. Microwaving the onions for a short time before grilling reduces the overall cooking time with tasty results. (Pictured on p. 48)

 4 **medium sweet yellow onions (7-8 ounces each)**

¼ **cup balsamic vinaigrette salad dressing or Italian salad dressing**

¼ **cup water**

⅓ **cup seasoned croutons, coarsely chopped**

1. Prepare grill for direct cooking over medium coals. Using **Chef's Knife**, cut ½-inch slice from top of each onion and just enough off root end so onion will stand upright on flat surface; peel. Using **Apple Wedger**, cut each onion into wedges from top to within ½ inch of root end; carefully remove wedger, keeping onion whole.

2. Cut four 12-inch squares of heavy-duty aluminum foil. Using **Pastry Brush**, brush foil lightly with some of the salad dressing; set aside. Place 2 of the onions and water in **Large Micro-Cooker®**; cover. Microwave on HIGH 3 minutes. Remove onions from micro-cooker using **Nylon Spoon**, reserving water. Place each onion on square of aluminum foil. Repeat with remaining onions.

3. Partially shape foil around each onion; do not seal. Brush onions evenly with remaining salad dressing. Bring foil up around onions; twist corners together to seal securely.

4. Place onions on grid of grill. Grill, uncovered, 15 minutes or until onions are tender. Remove from grill using **Barbecue Tongs**; open foil carefully to allow steam to escape. To serve, remove onions from foil; sprinkle evenly with croutons.

Yield: 4 servings

Nutrients per serving: Calories 100, Total Fat 5 g, Saturated Fat .5 g, Cholesterol 0 mg, Carbohydrate 13 g, Protein 2 g, Sodium 45 mg, Fiber 2 g

Diabetic exchanges per serving: ½ starch, 1 vegetable, 1 fat (½ carb)

Cook's Tips

▲ A sweet, pale yellow onion such as the Maui, Vidalia and Walla Walla is best for grilling. These special varieties are characteristically mild in flavor and exceedingly juicy. Choose onions that are evenly shaped with dry, papery skins. Avoid onions with soft spots. Always store onions in a cool, dry place.

▲ Use the **Food Chopper** to coarsely chop the croutons.

Great Grilled Vegetables

*From "A" for asparagus to "Z" for zucchini, you'll find a broad range of vegetables ideal for grilling whether over a bed of hot coals or in our **Professional Grill Pan**. Grilling intensifies the flavor of fresh vegetables making them well suited as a simple side or as part of a main dish entrée. Look to our handy chart below to provide you with reliable guidelines for preparing and cooking vegetables for optimal results.*

For Outdoor Charcoal Grilling:

1. Prepare grill for direct cooking over medium coals.
2. Prepare vegetable as directed below.
3. Brush vegetable with oil (except for corn on the cob); season with salt and black pepper, if desired.
4. Place vegetable on grid of grill.
5. Grill, uncovered, according to time indicated in chart or until crisp-tender.

For Indoor Grill Pan Cooking:

1. Prepare vegetable as directed below.
2. Heat pan 5 minutes over medium-high heat.
3. Spray vegetable with non-stick cooking spray or vegetable oil; season with salt and black pepper, if desired.
4. Place vegetable in pan.
5. Cook according to time indicated in chart or until crisp-tender.

Vegetable	Preparation	Outdoor/Charcoal Grill	Indoor/Grill Pan	Special Instructions
Asparagus	Cut off woody ends.	Grill 6-8 minutes.	Cook 10-12 minutes.	Turn frequently.
Bell Peppers	Cut into quarters.	Grill 6-8 minutes.	Cook 10-12 minutes.	Turn occasionally.
Corn on the Cob	Pull back husks; remove silk and rinse with water. Pull husks back up to cover corn.	Grill 20-22 minutes.	Not recommended	Turn occasionally.
Eggplant	Cut into ½-inch slices.	Grill 6-8 minutes.	Cook 6-9 minutes.	Turn occasionally.
Onions	Cut into ½-inch slices.	Grill 10-12 minutes.	Cook 10-12 minutes.	Turn once.
Portobello Mushrooms	Trim stem ends.	Grill 6-8 minutes.	Cook 6-8 minutes.	Turn occasionally.
Potatoes	Do not peel; cut into ½-inch slices (use Russet or Yukon Gold).	Grill 10-12 minutes.	Cook 10-14 minutes.	Turn occasionally.
Tomatoes	Cut in half.	Grill 6-8 minutes.	Cook 5-8 minutes.	Turn occasionally.
Yellow Summer Squash and Zucchini	Cut into ½-inch slices.	Grill 6-8 minutes.	Cook 6-9 minutes.	Turn occasionally.

Blue Ribbon Barbecue Sauces

Here's your chance to try out some of our first-rate barbecue sauces — thick, tomato-based sauces that range from sweet and tangy to hot and spicy — all developed to complement the flavor of beef, pork or poultry.

For Barbecue Sauce:

1. Heat oil in **Medium (3-qt.) Saucepan** over medium heat. Add onion and/or garlic. Cook 2 minutes or until tender.
2. Stir in remaining ingredients; return to a boil. Reduce heat to medium-low. Simmer, covered, 10 minutes.
3. Using **Barbecue Basting Brush**, brush barbecue sauce on food during the last 10-15 minutes of grilling to prevent burning.

Ingredients	Traditional	Asian	Berry-Citrus	Mexican	Sweet 'N Smoky
Oil	2 teaspoons vegetable oil	2 teaspoons dark sesame oil	2 teaspoons vegetable oil	2 teaspoons vegetable oil	2 teaspoons vegetable oil
Finely chopped onion and/or pressed garlic	¼ cup onion	¼ cup sliced green onions with tops 1 garlic clove, pressed	¼ cup onion	1 garlic clove, pressed	¼ cup onion
Ketchup	2 cups	2 cups	1½ cups	2 cups	1½ cups
Packed brown sugar	½ cup	½ cup	Omit	½ cup	Omit
Worcestershire sauce	3 tablespoons	Omit	1 tablespoon	3 tablespoons	3 tablespoons
Juice or vinegar	2 tablespoons lemon juice	2 tablespoons rice vinegar	2 tablespoons orange juice	¼ cup lime juice	2 tablespoons cider vinegar
Additional ingredients	Tabasco® hot pepper sauce to taste (optional)	3 tablespoons soy sauce 2 teaspoons finely chopped, peeled fresh gingerroot	Substitute 1 jar (12 ounces) seedless blackberry jam for the brown sugar 1 teaspoon Dijon mustard 2 teaspoons orange zest	1 can (4 ounces) chopped green chilies, drained 2 tablespoons chili powder 1½ teaspoons ground cumin	Substitute ½ cup honey for the brown sugar 2 tablespoons *Pantry Barbecue Seasoning* Mix 1 teaspoon prepared mustard
Yield	2⅔ cups	3 cups	2¾ cups	3 cups	2⅓ cups

Low Fat Nutrients per serving (2 tablespoons): Calories 50, Total Fat 1 g, Saturated Fat 0 g, Cholesterol 0 mg, Carbohydrate 12 g, Protein 0 g, Sodium 300 mg, Fiber 0 g
Diabetic exchanges per serving (2 tablespoons): 1 fruit (1 carb)

Cook's Tips

▲ These recipes have generous yields with enough sauce to serve at the table alongside your grilled foods. When getting ready to grill, portion out just the amount of sauce you need for brushing on your meat. This way the barbecue basting brush used on uncooked meat will not be in contact with the sauce being passed at the table. For maximum food safety, discard any remaining sauce used to baste raw meat.

▲ Refrigerate unused sauce, covered, up to 2 weeks.

Grilling Basics

Getting great results from your barbecue grill is easy once you've mastered the basics. Here we offer some techniques, tools and tips to help you get your grilling off to a successful start.

Types of Cooking

The cooking times suggested in the grilled recipes for this cookbook were arrived at using a 22½-inch diameter kettle-shaped grill with charcoal briquettes that have reached a medium cooking temperature. If you are cooking with a gas grill, your cooking times will be similar but possibly a bit longer. You'll want to consult the owner's manual for heating directions. Rest assured, the end results will be delicious, whichever type of grill you choose.

Prepare the grill for direct or indirect cooking according to the recipe directions, then light the coals. Once lighted, the briquettes will take about 20-30 minutes to become covered with pale gray ash. Carefully spread the coals onto the fire grate depending on the cooking method chosen, and you're ready to start grilling.

Direct Cooking

Direct cooking is cooking food directly over hot coals spread evenly over the fire grate in a single layer extending about 1 inch beyond the area of the food. This method is used for grilling foods that take less than 25 minutes to cook such as steaks, chops and burgers. Place the food on the grill grid directly above the coals and turn as recipe directs in order to expose both sides of the food to the heat.

Indirect Cooking

Indirect cooking is cooking food over a drip pan centered on the bottom of the fire grate with the hot coals spread to the sides of the kettle. This method is used for grilling larger cuts of meat that require longer cooking times. Position the grill grid so that additional coals can be added, if necessary. Place the food on the grill grid over the pan and cover the grill. Covering the grill makes it more oven-like, eliminating any need to turn the food. Be sure to resist the urge to peek at the food during cooking since heat will escape every time the grill lid is lifted.

Determining the Heat Level

To test the heat level of your coals, carefully place your palm above the coals at cooking height. Count the number of seconds you can hold your hand there before the heat makes you withdraw it. If you can keep it there for 3 seconds, the coals are medium-hot. At 4 seconds, the coals are at medium, and at 5 seconds they're at medium-low.

Grilling Tools from The Pampered Chef®

Quality barbecue tools are essential for making grilling easier. Our long-handled brush, turner, tongs and fork stay cool to the touch and allow you to keep a safe distance from the heat of the grill. Whether you're approaching the grill for the first time or you consider yourself a grill master, you'll appreciate these versatile grilling tools and helpful hints.

Barbecue Basting Brush

This wide brush with natural bristles is ideal for brushing sauces and marinades onto foods while they cook.

Barbecue Turner

The wide beveled edge of this heavy-duty stainless steel turner is best for turning burgers, steaks and delicate fish fillets. Be sure to slip the protective sleeve onto the head for safe storage.

Barbecue Tongs

The curved stainless steel scalloped edges are perfect for turning most foods or for moving foods on the grill.

Barbecue Fork

Use in combination with the turner to hold foods against the turner head or to lift foods from the grill. Avoid piercing meats while cooking so the flavorful juices aren't lost.

Barbecue Mitt

Our long, well-insulated suede mitt provides extra protection from the heat of the grill. Its exclusive design allows you to easily grip tools without slipping during use.

Clock/Timer

Take the guesswork out of grilling! Use the clock/timer to let you know when food needs to be checked, turned or taken off the grill.

Pocket Thermometer

Our instant-read thermometer allows you to check the internal temperature of meats to determine when food is cooked to a safe and/or desired degree of doneness.

Grilling Tips

- Use the cooking times in recipes and charts as guidelines. You'll need to allow more cooking time on cold or windy days and at higher altitudes, and less when the weather is very hot.
- Lightly coat the grill grid with vegetable oil or cooking spray before placing it over hot coals to keep foods from sticking. Never spray vegetable oil directly over hot coals.
- Trim excess fat from meats using the **Kitchen Shears**. Less fat is healthier and keeps flare-ups to a minimum.
- If flare-ups occur, quickly cover the grill with the lid. In addition, keep the **Kitchen Spritzer** (or a spray bottle) filled with water handy to mist any flare-ups that may char your food.
- Marinate foods in the refrigerator in resealable plastic food storage bags.
- If a marinade will also be used for brushing the meat during grilling, reserve part of the marinade for brushing before adding the remaining marinade to raw meat, poultry or fish. The same good food safety practice applies to a sauce that will be used for both brushing on meat during grilling and for passing at the table. Divide the sauce for the two uses before starting to cook.
- Always discard any leftover marinade or sauce used for brushing that was in contact with raw or partially cooked meat, poultry or fish.
- Always place cooked foods on a clean platter or **Cutting Board** to avoid cross-contamination from raw meats.

Cool Kitchen Cooking

Keep it cool with
quick-cooked meals
guaranteed to beat
the heat.

Southwestern Cobb Salad (p. 56)

Southwestern Cobb Salad

Prep, cook and chill time: 1 hour, 10 minutes

Put a southwestern spin on the traditional Cobb salad with this platter of inviting ingredients. Family members or dinner guests can make their salads just the way they like them. (Pictured on p. 54-55)

▲ To prepare hard-cooked eggs, place eggs in **Petite (1½-qt.) Saucepan**. Cover with water about 1 inch above eggs. Bring water to a boil. Remove saucepan from heat. Cover and let stand 20 minutes. Immediately run cold water into pan to cool eggs. Peel shells.

▲ Toss cubed avocado with a little fresh lime juice to prevent it from turning brown.

Dressing

- ¼ **cup milk**
- ⅓ **cup mayonnaise**
- ⅓ **cup sour cream**
- 1 **tablespoon lime juice**
- 1 **tablespoon *Pantry Southwestern Seasoning* Mix**

Salad

- 1 **pound boneless, skinless chicken breasts (about 3-4)**
- **Salt and ground black pepper**
- 1 **teaspoon vegetable oil**
- 3 **hard-cooked eggs, sliced**
- 1 **avocado, peeled and cubed**
- 1 **large red bell pepper, seeded and diced**
- 1 **cup canned black beans, rinsed and drained**
- 1 **package (10 ounces) torn romaine lettuce (8 cups)**
- ¼ **small red onion, cut into thin wedges**
- 6 **slices bacon, crisply cooked and cut up (optional)**

1. For dressing, pour milk into **Measure, Mix, & Pour™**. Add mayonnaise, sour cream, lime juice and seasoning mix; mix until well blended. Refrigerate at least 1 hour to allow flavors to blend.

2. Meanwhile, for salad, season chicken breasts with salt and black pepper. Heat oil in **Professional (10-in.) Skillet** over medium heat. Add chicken breasts; cook 5-7 minutes on each side or until chicken is no longer pink in the center. Remove chicken from skillet; cool slightly. Cut chicken diagonally into thin strips using **Chef's Knife**. Wrap tightly and refrigerate until ready to assemble salad.

3. Prepare hard-cooked eggs as directed in Cook's Tip. Slice eggs using **Egg Slicer Plus®**. Cut avocado in half; remove pit and peel. Cut avocado into ½-inch cubes and dice bell pepper. Drain and rinse beans in small **Colander**.

4. Place lettuce in serving bowl. Slice onion into thin wedges; toss with lettuce. Arrange remaining salad ingredients in rows on **Oval Platter**. To serve, top lettuce with salad ingredients using **Large Serving Tongs**. Drizzle with dressing.

Yield: 6 servings

Nutrients per serving: Calories 350, Total Fat 21 g, Saturated Fat 6 g, Cholesterol 170 mg, Carbohydrate 15 g, Protein 26 g, Sodium 360 mg, Fiber 7 g

Diabetic exchanges per serving: ½ starch, 4 meat, 2 fat (½ carb)

MENU SUGGESTION

Serve this salad with a basket of warm corn muffins, fresh pineapple spears sprinkled with toasted coconut and *Spiced Tropical Tea Cooler* (p. 101).

Taco-Topped Potatoes

Prep and cook time: 30 minutes

A seasoned ground beef mixture is the starting point for two quick family dinners. Serve hearty stuffed spuds with traditional taco toppers the first night and the all-time favorite, Sloppy Joes, the next. (Pictured on p. 59)

4 large baking potatoes (10-12 ounces each)

½ recipe prepared *Make-Ahead Seasoned Ground Beef* (see below)

¼ cup water

2 teaspoons chili powder

½ teaspoon ground cumin

½ cup (2 ounces) shredded Mexican cheese blend

Optional toppings: chopped tomatoes, sliced pitted ripe olives, sour cream and snipped fresh cilantro

1. Scrub potatoes; prick in several places using Hold 'N Slice™. Place in **Deep Dish Baker**. Microwave on HIGH 20-22 minutes or until tender, rotating and turning potatoes after 12 minutes.

2. Meanwhile, prepare ground beef mixture as recipe directs for *Make-Ahead Seasoned Ground Beef*. Add water, chili powder and cumin to half of ground beef mixture remaining in skillet. Cover and simmer over low heat 5 minutes.

3. Split potatoes lengthwise; squeeze gently and fluff with fork. Top with ground beef mixture, cheese and desired toppings.

Yield: 4 servings

Nutrients per serving: Calories 550, Total Fat 15 g, Saturated Fat 4 g, Cholesterol 55 mg, Carbohydrate 71 g, Protein 34 g, Sodium 720 mg, Fiber 7 g

Diabetic exchanges per serving: 4 starch, 3 meat, 1 vegetable (4 carb)

Cook's Tips

▲ The Mexican meat mixture is very versatile. For traditional tacos, fill warmed tortillas with the meat mixture. Add shredded Mexican cheese blend, any of the optional toppings and shredded lettuce, if desired.

▲ For taco salads, top torn salad greens with the meat mixture. Add shredded Mexican cheese blend, any of the optional toppings and tortilla chips, if desired.

Make-Ahead Seasoned Ground Beef

2 pounds lean (90%) ground beef

½ cup chopped onion

1 garlic clove, pressed

½ teaspoon salt

⅛ teaspoon ground black pepper

2 cans (8 ounces each) tomato sauce

1. Place ground beef in **Family (12-in.) Skillet**. Cook over medium heat 10-12 minutes or until no longer pink, breaking beef into crumbles; drain.

2. Add onion and garlic pressed with **Garlic Press**; sprinkle with salt and black pepper. Continue cooking 2-3 minutes or until onion is tender. Stir in tomato sauce. Remove skillet from heat.

3. Spoon half of mixture (about 2 cups) into refrigerator storage container. Cover and refrigerate for up to 2 days for use in *Sloppy Joe's Pocket Sandwiches* (p. 58). Use remaining half of mixture for *Taco-Topped Potatoes* (see above).

Cook's Tips

▲ When purchasing pita pocket bread, be sure to buy pita rounds that will form pockets when cut in half.

▲ This meat mixture can be used to fill hamburger buns or Kaiser rolls, too.

Sloppy Joe's Pocket Sandwiches

Prep and microwave time: 15 minutes

Sloppy Joes aren't so sloppy when they're served in pita bread pockets.

½ **recipe prepared *Make-Ahead Seasoned Ground Beef* (p. 57)**

2 **tablespoons ketchup**

1 **tablespoon packed brown sugar**

2 **teaspoons prepared mustard**

½ **teaspoon ground allspice (optional)**

2 **pita pocket bread rounds, cut in half**

4 **slices (¾ ounce each) American cheese, cut diagonally in half**

   Green bell pepper rings (optional)

1. Place prepared ground beef mixture in **Small Micro-Cooker®**. Stir in ketchup, brown sugar, mustard and allspice, if desired. Microwave, covered, on HIGH 4-5 minutes or until thoroughly heated, stirring after 2 minutes.

2. Wrap pita bread pockets in microwave-safe plastic wrap. Microwave on HIGH 30 seconds to soften. Place cheese slices in pockets. Fill with ground beef mixture. Garnish with bell pepper rings.

Yield: 4 sandwiches

Nutrients per serving: Calories 350, Total Fat 13 g, Saturated Fat 6 g, Cholesterol 50 mg, Carbohydrate 29 g, Protein 29 g, Sodium 1010 mg, Fiber 2 g

Diabetic exchanges per serving: 2 starch, 3 meat (2 carb)

MENU SUGGESTION

Look to the deli and produce sections of your local grocery store for a selection of quick accompaniments. Fruit salad, Kosher pickles or vegetable sticks would all be good choices.

Sloppy Joe's Pocket Sandwiches, Taco-Topped Potatoes (p. 57)

Cashew Chicken & Broccoli Stir-Fry

Prep time: 25 minutes   Cook time: 15-20 minutes

No one will mind eating veggies tonight — not when they're in a stir-fry with golden chicken, curly noodles and a flavorful sauce with a special ingredient...peanut butter.

Sauce

- ½ **cup fat-free chicken broth**
- ¼ **cup creamy peanut butter**
- 2 **tablespoons reduced-sodium soy sauce**
- 1 **tablespoon honey**
  Dash of ground red pepper

Vegetables and Chicken

- 4 **cups broccoli florets**
- 3 **stalks celery, cut diagonally into ½-inch slices**
- 3 **green onions with tops, cut into 1-inch pieces**
- 2 **teaspoons finely chopped, peeled fresh gingerroot, divided**
- 1 **pound boneless, skinless chicken breast halves, cut into 1-inch pieces**
- 4 **teaspoons vegetable oil, divided**
- 2 **garlic cloves, pressed, divided**
- 2 **packages (3 ounces each) ramen noodles, any flavor**
- ⅓ **cup cashews or peanuts**

1. For sauce, combine chicken broth, peanut butter, soy sauce, honey and ground red pepper in **Small Batter Bowl**; mix with **Stainless Steel Whisk** (mixture will not be smooth). Set aside.

2. For vegetables and chicken, cut broccoli, celery and green onions using **Chef's Knife**. Finely chop peeled fresh gingerroot using **Food Chopper**. Set vegetables aside. Cut chicken into 1-inch pieces.

3. Heat 2 teaspoons of the oil in **Stir-Fry Skillet** over high heat until hot. Add chicken, 1 teaspoon of the gingerroot and 1 garlic clove pressed with **Garlic Press**. Cook and stir 6-7 minutes or until chicken is no longer pink. Remove from skillet; keep warm.

4. Reduce heat to medium-high. Heat remaining 2 teaspoons oil in same skillet. Add broccoli, celery and remaining gingerroot and garlic. Cook and stir 2 minutes. Add green onions and continue cooking 2 minutes or until vegetables are crisp-tender. Return chicken to skillet. Stir in sauce; bring to a boil. Remove skillet from heat.

5. Meanwhile, bring 4 cups water to a boil in **Small (2-qt.) Saucepan**. Break noodles and add to boiling water (discard seasoning packets or reserve for another use). Cook 3 minutes, stirring occasionally; drain. Stir noodles into chicken mixture. Sprinkle with cashews. Serve immediately.

Yield: 4 servings

Nutrients per serving: Calories 540, Total Fat 22 g, Saturated Fat 3.5 g, Cholesterol 65 mg, Carbohydrate 50 g, Protein 41 g, Sodium 650 mg, Fiber 6 g

Diabetic exchanges per serving: 3 starch, 4½ meat (3 carb)

Cook's Tips

▲ The secret to successful stir-frying is having all of the ingredients sliced, chopped and measured before you begin to cook.

▲ The Pampered Chef **Bamboo Spatula Set** has been specially designed for stir-frying in the nonstick stir-fry skillet.

▲ When stir-frying the chicken, add chicken to the skillet and let it brown lightly before you start to stir. This will give the chicken nice color and added flavor.

▲ Always wash cutting board, knife and hands in hot, soapy water after cutting raw chicken. It's easiest and safest to cut up the vegetables before cutting the chicken.

MENU SUGGESTION

Assorted sliced fresh fruits, such as oranges, kiwis and strawberries, would make a colorful accompaniment. Don't forget the fortune cookies!

Italian Salad Pizza

Prep time: 15 minutes   Bake time: 12-14 minutes

30 Minutes or less

This flavorful pizza, topped with fresh salad ingredients, is best when served immediately.

Crust

1	**package (10 ounces) refrigerated pizza crust**
2	**garlic cloves, pressed**
½	**teaspoon dried oregano leaves**
¼	**teaspoon dried basil leaves**

Toppings

5	**cups thinly sliced romaine lettuce**
1	**medium tomato, seeded and diced**
½	**cup thinly sliced red onion**
¼	**cup pitted ripe olives, sliced**
¼	**cup fat-free Italian salad dressing**
1	**cup (4 ounces) shredded mozzarella cheese**
¼	**cup (1 ounce) grated fresh Parmesan cheese, divided**

1. Preheat oven to 425°F. For crust, roll out dough to edge of **Large Round Stone** using lightly floured **Baker's Roller™**. Press garlic over dough using **Garlic Press**; spread with **Skinny Scraper**. Sprinkle dough with oregano and basil. Bake on bottom rack of oven 12-14 minutes or until crust is golden brown.

2. Meanwhile, for toppings, slice lettuce and dice tomato using **Chef's Knife**. Using **Ultimate Slice & Grate** fitted with adjustable blade, thinly slice onion. Slice olives with **Egg Slicer Plus®**. Place lettuce, tomato, onion and olives in large **Colander Bowl**. Add dressing; toss to coat using **3-Way Tongs**.

3. Remove crust from oven to **Stackable Cooling Rack**. Immediately sprinkle with mozzarella cheese. Grate half of the Parmesan cheese over crust using **Deluxe Cheese Grater**. Top with salad mixture; grate remaining Parmesan cheese over pizza. Cut with **Pizza Cutter**; serve immediately.

Yield: 4 servings

Nutrients per serving: Calories 340, Total Fat 11 g, Saturated Fat 4.5 g, Cholesterol 20 mg, Carbohydrate 42 g, Protein 19 g, Sodium 1030 mg, Fiber 3 g

Diabetic exchanges per serving: 2 starch, 2 vegetable, 1½ meat (2 carb)

Cook's Tip

▲ Grating fresh Parmesan cheese over pizzas, pastas and salads is a quick way to add flavor to your cooking. Bring the **Deluxe Cheese Grater** right to the table for everyone to use.

MENU SUGGESTION

For a light summer meal, serve this pizza with colorful fresh fruit kebabs. Thread whole strawberries, pineapple chunks and melon balls on wooden skewers and serve with plain or vanilla low-fat yogurt for dipping.

Tuna Melt Patties

Prep time: 25 minutes   Cook time: 9-12 minutes

When the kids want burgers and you're tired of beef, try this grilled version of the ever-popular tuna salad sandwich. It's a lighter, healthier alternative that tastes good, too.

2 **cans (6 ounces each) water-packed white tuna, drained**
1/3 **cup finely chopped celery**
1/4 **cup green onions with tops, sliced**
1/4 **cup unseasoned dry bread crumbs**
2 **tablespoons light mayonnaise**
2 **tablespoons sweet pickle relish, drained**
1 **egg white**
1 **teaspoon prepared mustard**
4 **English muffins, split**
4 **slices (3/4 ounce each) reduced-fat American cheese**
   Additional light mayonnaise and prepared mustard (optional)
4 **lettuce leaves**
1 **tomato, sliced**

1. Drain tuna using small **Colander**; place tuna in small **Colander Bowl**. Flake tuna using **Pastry Blender**. Chop celery using **Food Chopper**. Slice green onions with **Utility Knife**. Add celery, green onions, dry bread crumbs, mayonnaise, pickle relish, egg white and mustard to tuna; mix well.

2. Heat **Professional Grill Pan** over medium heat 5 minutes. Place 2 English muffins, cut sides down, in pan. Toast 1-2 minutes; remove from pan. Repeat with remaining muffins. Set aside.

3. Form tuna mixture into 4 round patties, 1/2 inch thick. Lightly spray pan with vegetable oil using **Kitchen Spritzer**. Cook patties over medium heat 6 minutes, carefully turning with **Nylon Turner** after 3 minutes. Top with cheese. Continue cooking 1-2 minutes or until cheese is melted. Spread muffins with additional mayonnaise and mustard, if desired. Top 4 muffin halves with lettuce, tuna patties, tomato and remaining muffin halves.

Yield: 4 servings

Nutrients per serving: Calories 370, Total Fat 9 g, Saturated Fat 3 g, Cholesterol 50 mg, Carbohydrate 39 g, Protein 32 g, Sodium 1060 mg, Fiber 1 g

Diabetic exchanges per serving: 2 starch, 1 vegetable, 3 meat (2 carb)

Variation: *Swiss Salmon Burgers:* Substitute 2 cans (6 ounces each) boneless, skinless salmon for tuna, Dijon mustard for prepared mustard and Swiss cheese slices for American cheese. Omit pickle relish. Proceed as recipe directs.

Cook's Tips

▲ Use the **Egg Separator** to separate egg white from yolk.

▲ The **Large Scoop** is a handy tool for portioning the tuna mixture. Use 2 level scoops for each patty.

MENU SUGGESTION

Serve with baked tortilla or potato chips, assorted vegetable relishes and fresh apples or pears with a reduced-fat caramel sauce for dipping.

Philly Steak Wraps

Prep and cook time: 25 minutes Marinate time: 1-3 hours

Wrap it up! Traditional Philly sandwiches are transformed into tasty wraps with a contemporary twist.

▲ The Grill Pan is the perfect way to get delicious grilled flavor and attractive grill marks on food without setting foot out of the house. For best results, heat the pan over medium-high heat 5 minutes before adding food.

▲ Beef bouillon granules are the granular form of dehydrated bouillon cubes. If you do not have bouillon granules on hand, you can substitute 3 beef bouillon cubes for the granules called for in this recipe.

▲ From carving a simple steak to serving the holiday turkey, the Carving Set will get the job done beautifully. The set consists of both a carving knife and fork. It includes a storage case with built-in sharpening and honing mechanisms for perfect results every time.

1 **tablespoon beef bouillon granules**
1/2 **cup water**
3 **garlic cloves, pressed**
1/8 **teaspoon ground black pepper**
1 **boneless beef top sirloin steak, cut 1 inch thick (1 pound)**
1 **small green bell pepper, cut into 1/4-inch strips**
1 **small onion, cut into 1/4-inch slices Vegetable oil**
2 **cups (4 ounces) shredded mozzarella cheese**
4 **(9-10-inch) flour tortillas**

1. Combine bouillon granules, water, garlic pressed with **Garlic Press** and black pepper in **Small Batter Bowl**. Place marinade and steak in resealable plastic food storage bag; turn to coat. Marinate in refrigerator 1-3 hours, turning occasionally.

2. When ready to serve, cut bell pepper into 1/4-inch strips and onion into 1/4-inch slices using **Utility Knife**. Remove steak from marinade; lightly pat steak with paper towel to absorb some of the moisture. Discard marinade.

3. Heat **Professional Grill Pan** over medium-high heat 5 minutes. Place steak in pan; cook 6-8 minutes or until steak is medium rare (145°F) to medium (160°F) doneness, turning once using **Bamboo Tongs**. Remove steak to **Large Grooved Cutting Board**; cover loosely with aluminum foil.

4. Return pan to medium-high heat. Lightly spray pan with vegetable oil using **Kitchen Spritzer**. Add bell pepper and onion; cook 5-7 minutes or until vegetables are crisp-tender, turning occasionally. Remove vegetables to **Classic Batter Bowl**. Wipe pan with paper towel; set aside.

5. Using **Carving Set**, carve steak crosswise into thin slices. For each wrap, sprinkle 1/2 cup mozzarella cheese over tortilla. Place one fourth of the steak and vegetables in center; roll up tightly. Repeat with remaining tortillas, steak and vegetables.

6. Heat pan over medium-high heat until hot. Place wraps, seam side down, in pan. Spray tops of wraps lightly with vegetable oil; cook 2-3 minutes on each side or until grill marks appear deep golden brown. Remove wraps to cutting board; cut each wrap diagonally in half. Serve immediately.

Yield: 4 servings

Nutrients per serving (1 wrap): Calories 600, Total Fat 25 g, Saturated Fat 12 g, Cholesterol 145 mg, Carbohydrate 42 g, Protein 52 g, Sodium 740 mg, Fiber 2 g

Diabetic exchanges per serving (1 wrap): 2 1/2 starch, 1 vegetable, 6 meat (2 1/2 carb)

MENU SUGGESTION

Serve these hearty beef wraps with a colorful salad or a big bowl of your favorite soup.

Tortellini with Fresh Tomato Basil Sauce

30 Minutes or less

Prep and cook time: 25 minutes

When you've got a bumper crop of tomatoes on hand, savor this garden-fresh pasta sauce over cheese-stuffed pasta shapes.

1 package (20 ounces) uncooked refrigerated cheese-filled tortellini

6-8 medium tomatoes, seeded and coarsely chopped (3 cups)

3 tablespoons snipped fresh basil leaves

1 teaspoon balsamic vinegar

1/2 teaspoon salt

1/4 teaspoon ground black pepper

2 tablespoons olive oil

2 large garlic cloves, pressed

1/4 cup (1 ounce) grated fresh Parmesan cheese

1. Cook tortellini according to package directions in Dutch (6-qt.) Oven; drain in large Colander.

2. Meanwhile, core tomatoes with Cook's Corer™; cut tomatoes crosswise in half using Chef's Knife and remove seeds. Coarsely chop tomatoes; place in Small Batter Bowl.

3. Using Kitchen Shears, snip basil. Add basil, vinegar, salt and black pepper to tomatoes; mix gently with Small Mix 'N Scraper®.

4. Heat oil over medium heat in Dutch oven. Add garlic pressed with Garlic Press; stir 1 minute or until garlic is lightly browned. Remove Dutch oven from heat. Add tortellini and tomato mixture; toss gently. Spoon pasta into serving bowl. Grate Parmesan cheese using Deluxe Cheese Grater; sprinkle over pasta.

Yield: 4 servings

Nutrients per serving: Calories 510, Total Fat 16 g, Saturated Fat 5 g, Cholesterol 45 mg, Carbohydrate 73 g, Protein 21 g, Sodium 1100 mg, Fiber 6 g

Diabetic exchanges per serving: 4 starch, 1 meat, 1 fat, 1 vegetable (4 carb)

Cook's Tips

▲ Refrigerated and frozen pastas are considered fresh since they have not been dried and are not shelf stable. The cooking time is shorter than for dried pasta, so follow the package directions carefully.

▲ Two packages (9 ounces each) uncooked refrigerated cheese-filled tortellini or 1 package (19 ounces) uncooked frozen cheese-filled tortellini can be used in this recipe.

▲ During the summer, you'll want to use vine-ripened tomatoes for the best flavor. But, when tomatoes aren't in season, use plum tomatoes. To seed tomatoes, cut them crosswise in half. Gently squeeze each half, shaking out the seeds.

MENU SUGGESTION

A quick sauté of mixed garden veggies seasoned with fresh garlic and herbs and a loaf of warm Italian bread will complete this savory summertime meal.

Cook's Tips

▲ For added convenience, we've called for a rotisserie-cooked chicken, available at most large supermarkets. One cooked chicken weighs about 2 pounds and will yield about 3 cups of chopped meat.

▲ Our Pantry Barbecue Seasoning Mix adds extra smoky flavor to the barbecue sauce.

Saucy BBQ Chicken Sandwiches

Prep and cook time: 20 minutes

These sandwiches start with meat from a rotisserie-cooked chicken available in the deli at most large supermarkets. A sassy homemade sauce makes them extra special.

1 recipe **Blue Ribbon Barbecue Sauce, traditional flavor (p. 51)**

1 tablespoon **Pantry Barbecue Seasoning Mix (optional)**

1 **rotisserie-cooked chicken (2 pounds), skin and bones removed**

4 **Kaiser rolls, split**

1. Prepare barbecue sauce in **Medium (3-qt.) Saucepan** as recipe directs, adding seasoning mix, if desired.

2. Meanwhile, remove skin from chicken; discard skin. Remove meat from bones; discard bones. Pull and shred chicken using **Hold 'N Slice™**; cut into bite-size pieces. Add chicken to barbecue sauce; heat over medium heat 2-3 minutes or until heated through.

3. Split rolls using **Serrated Bread Knife**. Spoon chicken mixture over bottom halves of rolls using **Nylon Spoon**; cover with top halves.

Yield: 4 sandwiches

Nutrients per serving: Calories 630, Total Fat 11 g, Saturated Fat 2 g, Cholesterol 95 mg, Carbohydrate 98 g, Protein 38 g, Sodium 2110 mg, Fiber 3 g

Diabetic exchanges per serving: 6 starch, 1 vegetable, 2½ meat (6 carb)

MENU SUGGESTION

Pair this quick and easy supper sandwich with watermelon wedges, multigrain snack chips and your favorite relishes.

Sweet & Sour Shrimp Stir-Fry

Prep and cook time: 30 minutes

This colorful stir-fry features succulent shrimp, juicy pineapple and crisp-tender snow peas in a sweet-tangy sauce.

4 cups hot cooked rice
1/3 cup ketchup
3 tablespoons reduced-sodium soy sauce
2 tablespoons packed brown sugar
1 tablespoon white vinegar
4 teaspoons cornstarch
1 can (20 ounces) pineapple chunks in juice, undrained
8 ounces fresh snow pea pods, trimmed, cut diagonally in half (2 cups)
2 plum tomatoes, cut into wedges
2 teaspoons vegetable oil
2 garlic cloves, pressed
12 ounces frozen, cooked medium shrimp, thawed, rinsed and tails removed

1. Prepare rice in **Small (2-qt.) Saucepan** according to package directions. Meanwhile, in **Small Batter Bowl**, combine ketchup, soy sauce, brown sugar, vinegar and cornstarch; whisk using **Stainless Steel Whisk** until blended.

2. Drain pineapple in small **Colander**, reserving juice in small **Colander Bowl**. Measure 1/2 cup reserved pineapple juice; add to ketchup mixture in batter bowl and set aside. (Discard any remaining juice.)

3. Trim pea pods and cut diagonally in half using **Utility Knife**. Cut tomatoes into wedges.

4. Heat oil in **Stir-Fry Skillet** over medium-high heat until hot. Add pea pods and garlic pressed with **Garlic Press** to skillet. Using **Bamboo Spatulas**, stir-fry 1 minute. Reduce heat to medium. Stir ketchup mixture and add to skillet. Bring to a boil. Cook and stir 1 minute until thickened. Add pineapple and shrimp to skillet; toss to heat thoroughly. Remove from heat. Gently stir in tomatoes. Serve over rice.

Yield: 4 servings

Low Fat Nutrients per serving: Calories 520, Total Fat 5 g, Saturated Fat .5 g, Cholesterol 160 mg, Carbohydrate 87 g, Protein 30 g, Sodium 860 mg, Fiber 4 g

Diabetic exchanges per serving: 5 1/2 starch, 1/2 meat (5 1/2 carb)

Cook's Tips

▲ One large green bell pepper, cut into 1-inch pieces, can be substituted for the pea pods, if desired.

▲ Rice vinegar can be substituted for white vinegar. It is a mild, slightly sweet vinegar made from fermented rice that is popular in Asian cooking. It can be found in the Asian food section of most supermarkets.

MENU SUGGESTION

Your favorite flavor of frozen sherbet or sorbet sprinkled with fresh summer berries and served with almond cookies and tea would go nicely with this one-dish meal.

▲ To easily slice
avocado, begin by
cutting avocado in half,
avoiding pit. Twist and
separate halves.
Remove pit by carefully
striking center of pit
with **Chef's Knife** then
twisting knife to remove
pit. Holding one half of
the avocado in the palm
of your hand, slice
avocado lengthwise
using the tip of a spoon.
Do not cut through the
skin. The avocado slices
can be easily removed
with the spoon and can
be placed directly onto
the top of your
sandwiches.

▲ A firm-textured
Italian bread can be
substituted for the
sourdough bread,
if you prefer.

Grilled Chicken & Veggie Sandwiches

Prep time: 30 minutes   Cook time: 14-20 minutes

There's nothing ho-hum about this chicken sandwich. Grilled sourdough bread, a creamy ranch spread and crunchy vegetables piled high make this one sensational supper sandwich.

4   **ounces reduced-fat cream cheese (Neufchâtel), softened**
1   **tablespoon milk**
1   **packet (1 ounce) dry ranch dressing mix, divided**
1   **small garlic clove, pressed**
4   **boneless, skinless chicken breasts (about 4 ounces each)**
8   **slices (1/2 inch thick) sourdough bread**
    Vegetable oil
2   **tablespoons all-purpose flour**
1/2 **small cucumber, sliced**
2   **plum tomatoes, sliced**
1/2 **cup sliced red onion**
1   **carrot, cut into julienne strips**
1   **cup alfalfa sprouts**
1   **firm, ripe avocado, sliced**

1. In **Small Batter Bowl**, combine cream cheese, milk, 2 teaspoons of the dressing mix and garlic pressed with **Garlic Press**; mix well and set aside.

2. Place each chicken breast between 2 pieces of **Parchment Paper**. Flatten chicken to 3/4-inch thickness by alternately pounding and rolling with **Baker's Roller™**.

3. Heat **Professional Grill Pan** over medium heat 5 minutes. Lightly spray one side of each bread slice with vegetable oil using **Kitchen Spritzer**. Place half of slices, oiled side down, in pan. Cook 2-3 minutes on oiled side or until toasted. Remove bread slices to **Stackable Cooling Rack**. Repeat with remaining bread slices.

4. Combine remaining dressing mix and flour in **Flour/Sugar Shaker**; mix well. Sprinkle chicken evenly on both sides with flour mixture shaking off excess; lightly spray chicken with oil. Place chicken in pan; cook over medium heat 5-7 minutes per side until chicken is no longer pink in the center. Remove from pan; cool slightly. Refrigerate while preparing vegetables.

5. Score cucumber lengthwise using **Lemon Zester/Scorer**. Remove seeds using **The Corer™**. Using **Ultimate Slice & Grate** fitted with v-shaped blade, thinly slice cucumber, tomatoes and onion. Cut carrot into julienne strips using **Julienne Peeler**.

6. To assemble sandwiches, spread cream cheese mixture onto untoasted side of each bread slice using **Small Spreader**. On 4 of the bread slices, evenly layer cucumber, tomato, onion, chicken, carrot, alfalfa sprouts and avocado. Top with remaining bread slices, pressing firmly. Slice sandwiches diagonally in half using **Serrated Bread Knife**. Serve immediately.

Yield: 4 servings

Nutrients per serving: Calories 450, Total Fat 14 g, Saturated Fat 5 g, Cholesterol 80 mg, Carbohydrate 43 g, Protein 36 g, Sodium 1020 mg, Fiber 7 g

Diabetic exchanges per serving: 2 starch, 4 meat, 1 vegetable (2 carb)

Seafood Caesar Pasta Salad

Prep and cook time: 30 minutes   Chill time: 2-3 hours

Enjoy the robust flavors of traditional Caesar salad in a new version featuring penne pasta and crabmeat.

10 **ounces uncooked penne pasta (3 cups)**

1 **package (8 ounces) imitation crabmeat, cut into 1-inch pieces**

1/2 **cup diced red or green bell pepper**

2 **hard-cooked eggs, chopped**

1/4 **cup chopped red onion**

1/4 **cup (1 ounce) grated fresh Parmesan cheese**

2 **tablespoons snipped fresh parsley**

1 **bottle (8 ounces) reduced-fat creamy Caesar salad dressing**

6 **cups thinly sliced romaine lettuce**

1. Cook pasta according to package directions in **Professional (4-qt.) Casserole**; drain and rinse under cold running water using large **Colander**. Place pasta in large **Colander Bowl** and set aside.

2. Meanwhile, cut crabmeat into 1-inch pieces and dice bell pepper using **Chef's Knife**. Chop eggs and red onion using **Food Chopper**. Grate Parmesan cheese with **Deluxe Cheese Grater**. Snip parsley with **Kitchen Shears**. Add crabmeat, bell pepper, eggs, onion, cheese and parsley to pasta in bowl. Pour salad dressing over pasta mixture; mix well. Cover; refrigerate 2-3 hours to allow flavors to blend.

3. To serve, fill serving bowl with lettuce. Spoon pasta salad into center of bowl. Serve using **3-Way Tongs**.

Yield: 6 servings

Nutrients per serving: Calories 260, Total Fat 6 g, Saturated Fat 1.5 g, Cholesterol 75 mg, Carbohydrate 42 g, Protein 10 g, Sodium 530 mg, Fiber 3 g

Diabetic exchanges per serving: 2 starch, 2 vegetable, 1 fat (2 carb)

Variation: *Chicken Caesar Pasta Salad:* Substitute 2 cups chopped cooked chicken for the crabmeat. Proceed as recipe directs.

Cook's Tips

▲ When making pasta salads, it's a good idea to rinse the cooked pasta under cold running water to wash off the starch and keep the pasta from sticking together.

▲ To prepare hard-cooked eggs, see Cook's Tip on p. 56.

▲ To easily slice romaine lettuce, stack 3-4 lettuce leaves on top of each other; cut into thin strands using chef's knife.

MENU SUGGESTION

Serve this light salad with crusty Italian bread or crisp bread sticks.

Santa Fe Turkey Sauté

Prep time: 15 minutes   Cook time: 8 minutes

Two minutes per side is all that's needed to sauté these thin slices of cornmeal-coated turkey breast. Chopped fresh peaches add the sweet taste of summer to a jarred salsa topping.

1	**medium peach, peeled and coarsely chopped**
1	**tablespoon snipped fresh cilantro**
¾	**cup thick and chunky salsa**
¼	**cup yellow cornmeal**
2	**tablespoons all-purpose flour**
¾	**teaspoon ground cumin**
¾	**teaspoon salt**
¼	**teaspoon garlic powder**
⅛	**teaspoon ground black pepper**
1-1¼	**pounds turkey breast slices (about 6-7 slices)**
2	**teaspoons vegetable oil, divided**

1. Coarsely chop peach using **Food Chopper**. Snip cilantro using **Kitchen Shears**. In **Small Batter Bowl**, combine peach, cilantro and salsa; set aside.

2. In shallow dish, combine cornmeal, flour, cumin, salt, garlic powder and black pepper. Coat both sides of each turkey slice with cornmeal mixture. Discard any remaining cornmeal mixture.

3. In **Family (12-in.) Skillet**, heat 1 teaspoon of the oil over medium heat until hot. Add half of the turkey slices. Cook 2 minutes; turn using **Nylon Turner**. Continue cooking 2 minutes or until coating is golden brown and turkey is no longer pink. Remove turkey from skillet onto serving platter; keep warm. Cook remaining turkey slices in remaining 1 teaspoon oil. To serve, top with peach salsa.

Yield: 4 servings

Nutrients per serving: Calories 220, Total Fat 3.5 g, Saturated Fat .5 g, Cholesterol 70 mg, Carbohydrate 17 g, Protein 29 g, Sodium 820 mg, Fiber 1 g

Diabetic exchanges per serving: 1 starch, 4 meat (1 carb)

Cook's Tip

▲ For a really quick dinner, prepare salsa and coating mix earlier in the day. Cover and refrigerate salsa until ready to use. Cover coating mix until ready to coat turkey slices.

MENU SUGGESTION

Complete your menu with a seasoned rice mix and steamed green beans.

Vegetable Primavera

Prep and cook time: 25 minutes

Fresh garden vegetables add seasonal freshness and flavor to a packaged cheesy pasta mix.

Cook's Tips

▲ This recipe starts with a convenient packaged mix of dried pasta and cheese sauce. You'll find this product among the many pasta and rice products in most grocery stores.

▲ Get a jump start in preparing this recipe. Early in the day or the night before, cut vegetables, wrap securely and refrigerate so they're all ready when you begin the cooking.

3   cups broccoli florets
½   cup coarsely chopped red bell pepper
2   medium carrots, cut into ¼-inch slices (⅔ cup)
1   can (14½ ounces) reduced-sodium, fat-free chicken broth
1   cup water
1   cup milk
2   tablespoons butter or margarine
2   packages (4.4 - 4.7 ounces each) egg noodles Alfredo or fettuccine Alfredo
1   garlic clove, pressed
     Grated fresh Parmesan cheese (optional)

1. Cut broccoli into florets and coarsely chop bell pepper using **Chef's Knife**. Using **Crinkle Cutter**, cut carrots diagonally into ¼-inch slices.

2. In **Professional (4-qt.) Casserole**, bring chicken broth, water, milk and butter just to a boil. Stir in pasta and sauce mix; reduce heat to medium. Gently boil, uncovered, 5 minutes.

3. Stir in broccoli, bell pepper, carrots and garlic pressed with **Garlic Press**. Return to a boil and continue cooking 2 minutes. (Sauce will be thin. Do not overcook.) Let stand 8 minutes for sauce to thicken.

4. Spoon onto **Oval Platter**. Top with Parmesan cheese grated with **Deluxe Cheese Grater**, if desired.

Yield: 4 servings

Nutrients per serving: Calories 370, Total Fat 14 g, Saturated Fat 8 g, Cholesterol 95 mg, Carbohydrate 48 g, Protein 15 g, Sodium 1250 mg, Fiber 4 g

Diabetic exchanges per serving: 3 starch, 1 meat, 1 fat (3 carb)

MENU SUGGESTION

Homemade *Fresh Strawberry Pie* (p. 103) served with creamy whipped topping would be a delightful ending to a family meal.

Monte Cristo Sandwiches

Prep time: 15 minutes   Cook time: 5 minutes

Kids will love this French toast sandwich made with a melted cheese and mild ham filling.

2   **eggs**
¼   **cup milk**
8   **slices (½ inch thick) Italian bread**
8   **slices (½ ounce each) Swiss cheese**
6   **ounces thinly sliced deli ham or turkey or combination of both**
1   **tablespoon butter or margarine**
    Powdered sugar (optional)
½   **cup strawberry preserves**

1. In **Small Batter Bowl**, combine eggs and milk; whisk until smooth using **Stainless Steel Whisk**. Pour egg mixture into shallow bowl. Dip one side of 4 bread slices in egg mixture. Place bread, egg side down, on **Large Grooved Cutting Board**.

2. For each sandwich, place 1 cheese slice on bread. Top with 1½ ounces ham and additional cheese slice. Dip one side of remaining bread slices in egg mixture; top sandwiches, egg side up.

3. Melt butter in **Family (12-in.) Skillet** over medium heat. Cook sandwiches about 2 minutes on each side or until golden brown, turning with **Nylon Turner**. To serve, sprinkle sandwiches with powdered sugar using **Flour/Sugar Shaker**, if desired. Serve with strawberry preserves for dipping.

Yield: 4 sandwiches

Nutrients per serving: Calories 430, Total Fat 17 g, Saturated Fat 9 g, Cholesterol 170 mg, Carbohydrate 48 g, Protein 23 g, Sodium 850 mg, Fiber 1 g

Diabetic exchanges per serving: 3 starch, 2 meat, 1 fat (3 carb)

Cook's Tips

▲ The Monte Cristo is a diner classic. Although the sandwich is usually grilled or fried in butter, some restaurants batter and deep-fry it. Grilled or deep-fried, a Monte Cristo sandwich is not complete unless it is served with preserves, jam or jelly.

▲ American cheese can be substituted for the Swiss cheese, if desired.

▲ The **Square (11-in.) Griddle** can also be used to grill these sandwiches.

Italian Chicken Pasta Toss

Prep time: 20 minutes   Cook time: 15-20 minutes

Stir-fry cooking is the speedy method used to make this fresh Italian pasta dish. Bow tie pasta adds a kid-friendly touch, but feel free to substitute any favorite pasta shape.

6 **ounces uncooked bow tie pasta (about 3 cups)**

2 **plum tomatoes, seeded and diced**

1 **small onion, chopped**

1 **medium zucchini, sliced**

1 **small yellow or red bell pepper, cut into thin strips**

½ **pound boneless, skinless chicken breasts, cut into 1-inch strips**

2 **teaspoons olive oil**

2 **large garlic cloves, pressed**

½ **cup frozen peas**

1 **teaspoon Pantry Italian Seasoning Mix**

1 **teaspoon salt**

1 **ounce (¼ cup) grated fresh Parmesan cheese (optional)**

1. Cook pasta according to package directions in **Professional (4-qt.) Casserole**; drain and keep warm.

2. Meanwhile, dice tomatoes using **Chef's Knife** and chop onion with **Food Chopper**. Slice zucchini with **Crinkle Cutter**. Cut bell pepper into thin strips and chicken crosswise into 1-inch strips using **Utility Knife**.

3. Heat oil in **Stir-Fry Skillet** over medium-high heat until hot. Press garlic into skillet using **Garlic Press**. Add chicken. Stir-fry 5 minutes or until chicken is no longer pink, turning with **Bamboo Spatulas**. Reduce heat to medium. Add onion, zucchini, bell pepper, peas, seasoning mix and salt; stir-fry 2 minutes. Add tomatoes; heat 1-2 minutes, stirring gently until heated through. Remove from heat.

4. Stir in warm pasta. Grate Parmesan cheese with **Deluxe Cheese Grater**; sprinkle over pasta. Serve immediately.

Yield: 6 servings

Low Fat Nutrients per serving: Calories 190, Total Fat 3 g, Saturated Fat 0 g, Cholesterol 20 mg, Carbohydrate 27 g, Protein 14 g, Sodium 430 mg, Fiber 3 g

Diabetic exchanges per serving: 1½ starch, 1 meat (1½ carb)

MENU SUGGESTION

Garlic bread (see Cook's Tip, p. 25) would be tasty with this pasta dish. Serve fresh grapes and an assortment of natural cheeses for dessert.

Curried Vegetable Couscous

Prep and cook time: 30 minutes

Vegetarians and meat-eaters alike will enjoy this meatless main dish that takes just minutes to prepare. A sprinkling of curry powder and cumin lends exotic flair.

1 **can (14½ ounces) vegetable broth**
1 **cup plain couscous**
1 **medium carrot, grated**
1 **small yellow summer squash, sliced and cut in half**
1 **small zucchini, sliced and cut in half**
½ **cup finely chopped red onion**
2 **garlic cloves, pressed**
2 **teaspoons olive oil**
1 **can (15 ounces) garbanzo beans, drained and rinsed**
⅓ **cup golden raisins**
½ **teaspoon *each* curry powder, ground cumin and salt**
¼ **teaspoon red pepper flakes**
4 **large red bell peppers, halved and steamed (see Cook's Tip)**
  Snipped fresh parsley

1. In Small (2-qt.) Saucepan, bring vegetable broth to a boil. Add couscous; cover and remove from heat. Let stand 5 minutes.

2. Using **Ultimate Slice & Grate**, grate carrot. Slice yellow squash and zucchini; cut slices in half. Finely chop onion using **Food Chopper**. Place vegetables in **Classic Batter Bowl**; press garlic into batter bowl using **Garlic Press**.

3. In Large (10-in.) Skillet, heat oil over medium-high heat until hot. Add vegetables; cook 5-6 minutes, stirring occasionally or until vegetables are crisp-tender. Stir in garbanzo beans, raisins, curry powder, cumin, salt and red pepper flakes; mix thoroughly with **Classic Scraper**. Add couscous; continue cooking 1-2 minutes or until heated through. Spoon couscous mixture into bell pepper halves. Sprinkle with parsley.

Yield: 4 servings

Nutrients per serving: Calories 360, Total Fat 5 g, Saturated Fat 0 g, Cholesterol 0 mg, Carbohydrate 71 g, Protein 12 g, Sodium 910 mg, Fiber 10 g

Diabetic exchanges per serving: 4 starch (4 carb)

Cook's Tips

▲ To steam bell peppers, place 6 cups water in **Professional (8-qt.) Stockpot**. Place **Steamer Insert** in stockpot; cover and bring water to a boil. Cut bell peppers in half, leaving stem intact; remove seeds and membranes. Arrange bell pepper halves upright in steamer; cover and cook 6-8 minutes or until crisp-tender. Remove using **Nylon Tongs**.

▲ Look for packages of couscous in the rice or pasta section of the supermarket. Couscous or granular semolina is made from durum wheat, the main ingredient in good pastas. This quick-cooking pasta is small and bead shaped. Use plain couscous, not a flavored mix, for this recipe.

MENU SUGGESTION

Complement this delicious meatless main dish with a crisp green salad, flat bread or warm pita bread and feta cheese slices.

▲ This salad can be prepared up to 1 day in advance.

▲ For a pleasing side-dish salad that complements grilled pork or poultry, omit the turkey.

▲ Firm tofu, cut into cubes, makes an excellent substitute for the poultry in this recipe.

▲ Vermicelli is long, thin pasta similar to thin spaghetti.

Asian Summer Salad

Prep and cook time: 50 minutes   Chill time: 1 hour

You can prepare this main-dish salad in the morning, then enjoy a relaxing afternoon at the beach knowing dinner is waiting in the fridge.

Salad

- **8 ounces uncooked vermicelli pasta**
- **¾ cup julienne-cut carrots, 2 inches long**
- **¾ cup julienne-cut zucchini, 2 inches long**
- **¾ cup chopped red bell pepper**
- **⅓ cup sliced green onions with tops**
- **¾ pound deli roast turkey or chicken breast, cut ½ inch thick**

Dressing

- **¼ cup vegetable oil**
- **3 tablespoons rice vinegar**
- **3 tablespoons reduced-sodium soy sauce**
- **2 teaspoons sugar**
- **⅛ teaspoon ground red pepper**
- **1 teaspoon finely chopped, peeled fresh gingerroot**
- **1 garlic clove, pressed**
- **Coarsely chopped peanuts or cashews and fresh cilantro (optional)**

1. For salad, break vermicelli into quarters. Cook according to package directions in **Professional (4-qt.) Casserole**; drain and rinse under cold running water using large **Colander**. Place vermicelli in large **Colander Bowl** and set aside.

2. Using **Julienne Peeler**, cut carrots and zucchini into julienne strips; cut strips into 2-inch pieces using **Chef's Knife**. Chop bell pepper and slice green onions. Cut turkey into thin pieces, 2 inches long. Add vegetables and turkey to vermicelli.

3. For dressing, combine oil, vinegar, soy sauce, sugar and ground red pepper in **Small Batter Bowl**. Peel gingerroot; finely chop using **Food Chopper**. Add gingerroot and garlic pressed with **Garlic Press** to batter bowl. Mix well using **Stainless Steel Whisk**. Pour dressing over salad; toss with **3-Way Tongs**. Cover and refrigerate at least 1 hour to allow flavors to blend. Spoon salad into serving bowl. Garnish with chopped peanuts and cilantro, if desired.

Yield: 6 servings

Nutrients per serving (1⅔ cups): Calories 300, Total Fat 11 g, Saturated Fat 1.5 g, Cholesterol 25 mg, Carbohydrate 35 g, Protein 16 g, Sodium 980 mg, Fiber 2 g

Diabetic exchanges per serving (1⅔ cups): 2 starch, 1½ meat, ½ fat (2 carb)

MENU SUGGESTION

Crisp sesame breadsticks, melon wedges and orange sherbet are perfect accompaniments to this Asian-inspired salad.

Pepperoni Pizzadillas

Prep time: 20 minutes   Cook time: 12-14 minutes

The pizzadilla is the Italian spin-off of the quesadilla. These fun sandwiches will be a welcome addition to soup at lunchtime.

1 package (8 ounces) shredded Italian cheese blend
1 teaspoon dried oregano leaves
1 garlic clove, pressed
1 cup tomato, seeded and coarsely chopped
1½ cups chopped vegetables such as green bell peppers, mushrooms or pitted ripe olives
¼ cup thinly sliced green onions with tops (optional)
4 (9-10-inch) flour tortillas
30 slices pepperoni
½ cup refrigerated marinara sauce, warmed

1. In **Small Batter Bowl**, combine cheese, oregano and garlic pressed with **Garlic Press**. Coarsely chop tomato and bell peppers with **Chef's Knife**. Chop mushrooms and olives with **Food Chopper**. Thinly slice green onions with chef's knife, if desired.

2. To assemble each pizzadilla, place 1 tortilla on flat side of **Large Grooved Cutting Board**. Sprinkle evenly with ½ cup of the cheese mixture, half of the pepperoni and ½ cup tomato. Top with ¾ cup of the remaining vegetables and 2 tablespoons of the green onions, if desired. Sprinkle with an additional ½ cup of the cheese mixture; top with second tortilla. Repeat with remaining ingredients to assemble second pizzadilla.

3. Heat **Professional Grill Pan** over medium heat 5 minutes. Carefully slide 1 pizzadilla into pan using **Nylon Turner**. Cook 3-5 minutes or until grill marks on bottom tortilla are dark golden brown and tortilla is crisp. Carefully slide pizzadilla from pan onto large dinner plate. Place second dinner plate upside down over pizzadilla, firmly hold plates together, and turn over so that grilled side is on top.

4. Return pan to heat; gently slide pizzadilla, uncooked side down, back into pan. Cook 3 minutes or until grill marks on second side are dark golden brown and tortilla is crisp. Slide onto serving platter. Grill second pizzadilla as directed above. Cut into wedges using **Pizza Cutter**. Serve with warm marinara sauce.

Yield: 4 servings

Nutrients per serving: Calories 600, Total Fat 29 g, Saturated Fat 14 g, Cholesterol 41 mg, Carbohydrate 48 g, Protein 39 g, Sodium 1760 mg, Fiber 5 g

Diabetic exchanges per serving: 3 starch, 4 meat, 1 fat (3 carb)

Variation: *Sausage Pizzadillas:* Substitute ½ pound Italian sausage, crumbled, cooked and drained, for pepperoni, if desired.

Cook's Tips

▲ You will find refrigerated marinara sauce in the refrigerated fresh pasta or Italian food section of the supermarket.

▲ Your favorite pizza sauce or spaghetti sauce can be substituted for the refrigerated marinara sauce.

▲ You can choose any combination of vegetables to fill your pizzadillas.

▲ Arborio rice is a short-grain Italian rice traditionally used for risotto. Its high starch content gives risotto its creamy texture.

▲ Substitute 1-2 cups chopped cooked chicken or turkey for the ham, if you like.

Easy Risotto with Ham and Peas

Prep and microwave time: 35-38 minutes

You'll love this creamy Italian rice dish accented with fresh Parmesan cheese. Easy microwave directions eliminate the need for constant stirring.

2 cans (14½ ounces each) reduced-sodium, fat-free chicken broth
½ cup water
½ cup chopped onion
1⅓ cups uncooked arborio rice
3 tablespoons olive oil
1 ham slice (8 ounces)
½ cup frozen peas, thawed
½ cup (2 ounces) grated fresh Parmesan cheese, divided
2 tablespoons snipped fresh parsley
Coarsely ground black pepper

1. Combine chicken broth and water in **Large Micro-Cooker®**. Microwave on HIGH 3 minutes until very warm; set aside.

2. Meanwhile, chop onion using **Food Chopper**. Place onion and rice in **Deep Dish Baker**. Drizzle with oil; stir until rice is coated using **Small Mix 'N Scraper®**. Microwave 4 minutes, stirring well after 2 minutes.

3. Gradually stir warm broth into rice mixture. Microwave, uncovered, 10 minutes; stir. Continue microwaving 8-11 minutes or until most of the liquid is absorbed. Remove baker from oven.

4. Meanwhile, cut ham into short, thin pieces using **Utility Knife**. Place frozen peas in small **Colander** and rinse under cold running water to thaw. Grate Parmesan cheese using **Deluxe Cheese Grater**. Snip parsley using **Kitchen Shears**.

5. Stir ham into rice mixture. Cover loosely with aluminum foil and let stand 5 minutes to allow rice to absorb remaining liquid. Stir in peas, half of the cheese and parsley. Garnish servings with remaining cheese and black pepper coarsely ground with **Salt and Pepper Mill**.

Yield: 4 servings

Nutrients per serving: Calories 510, Total Fat 16 g, Saturated Fat 4.5 g, Cholesterol 35 mg, Carbohydrate 65 g, Protein 23 g, Sodium 1340 mg, Fiber 3 g

Diabetic exchanges per serving: 4 starch, 1½ meat, 1 fat (4 carb)

MENU SUGGESTION

Foccacia bread and a salad of crisp greens, fresh tomato wedges and Italian dressing are all that's needed to complete this meal.

Pan-Seared Salmon with Julienne Vegetables

Prep time: 20 minutes   Cook time: 8-9 minutes

Firm-textured salmon is perfect for grilling indoors in our Professional Grill Pan. The julienne vegetable medley cooks quickly in the same pan.

2 **large carrots**
2 **medium yellow summer squash**
2 **medium zucchini**
3 **tablespoons butter or margarine**
2 **tablespoons snipped fresh parsley**
2 **garlic cloves, pressed**
½ **teaspoon salt**
⅛ **teaspoon ground black pepper**
4 **skinless salmon fillets (4-6 ounces each), about 1 inch thick**

1. Peel carrots. Cut carrots, yellow summer squash and zucchini into long julienne strips using **Julienne Peeler**, avoiding seeds, to measure 4 cups vegetables.

2. In **Small Micro-Cooker®**, microwave butter on HIGH 30 seconds or until melted. Stir in parsley snipped with **Kitchen Shears**, garlic pressed with **Garlic Press**, salt and black pepper. Reserve 1 tablespoon butter mixture. Using **Pastry Brush**, brush salmon fillets with remaining butter mixture.

3. Heat **Professional Grill Pan** over medium heat 5 minutes. Add vegetables and reserved 1 tablespoon butter mixture; toss to coat using **Bamboo Spatulas**. Cook and stir 2 minutes or until vegetables are crisp-tender; remove from pan and keep warm.

4. Return pan to heat. Increase heat to medium-high. Place salmon in pan; cook 3 minutes. Turn with **Nylon Turner**; cook 3-4 minutes or until salmon flakes easily with fork. Serve over vegetables.

Yield: 4 servings

Nutrients per serving: Calories 330, Total Fat 19 g, Saturated Fat 8 g, Cholesterol 90 mg, Carbohydrate 12 g, Protein 30 g, Sodium 460 mg, Fiber 4 g

Diabetic exchanges per serving: ½ starch, 4 meat (½ carb)

Cook's Tips

▲ Fresh fish should be refrigerated promptly after purchasing and used within 1-2 days.

▲ Salmon fillets are often sold with the skin intact. You can ask at the fish counter to have the skin removed. To remove the skin yourself, place fillet, skin side down, on **Cutting Board**. At one end, cut through to the skin using **Chef's Knife**. While firmly holding onto the skin, angle the knife and cut the flesh from the skin using a sawing motion.

▲ Test fish for doneness by flaking with a fork at its thickest point. It should be opaque throughout.

▲ To cook the salmon fillets over charcoal, prepare grill for direct cooking over medium coals. Brush fillets with butter mixture as recipe directs. Grill, covered, 8-10 minutes or until fish turns opaque and flakes easily with a fork.

Sweet Sensations

Satisfy your desire for quick, easy and refreshing summertime treats.

Banana Cream Brownie Squares (p. 98)

▲ To make chocolate curls, you'll need 1 square (1 ounce) semi-sweet chocolate for baking. Hold the **Vegetable Peeler** across the narrow side of the chocolate. Using even pressure, push the blade away from you to create curls. Or, grate chocolate over dessert using the **Deluxe Cheese Grater**.

▲ This dessert can be prepared through Step 3 several hours in advance. Just before serving, garnish as recipe directs in Step 4.

Banana Cream Brownie Squares

Prep time: 25 minutes   Bake time: 30-35 minutes   Cool time: 1 hour   Chill time: 30 minutes

Brownies topped with a creamy vanilla pudding mixture and fresh fruit are irresistible! (Pictured on p. 96-97)

¾ **cup dry roasted peanuts, chopped, divided**

1 **package (15-17 ounces) brownie mix (plus ingredients to make brownies)**

3 **medium bananas, divided**

1 **package (5.1 ounces) vanilla instant pudding and pie filling**

1¼ **cups cold milk**

1 **container (8 ounces) frozen whipped topping, thawed, divided**

12 **strawberries**

Chocolate curls (optional)

1. Preheat oven to 350°F. Using **Food Chopper**, chop peanuts. Prepare brownie mix according to package directions; stir in ½ cup of the peanuts. Pour into **Square Baker**. Bake according to package directions. Cool completely.

2. Using **Egg Slicer Plus®**, slice 2 of the bananas; place in single layer over brownie. In **Classic Batter Bowl**, whisk pudding mix into milk using **Stainless Steel Whisk**; beat until mixture just begins to thicken. Using **Classic Scraper**, gently fold in 2½ cups of the whipped topping. Quickly spread pudding mixture over bananas. Refrigerate 30 minutes.

3. Sprinkle remaining ¼ cup peanuts over pudding mixture. Attach open star tip to **Easy Accent® Decorator**; fill with remaining whipped topping. Cut dessert into squares; garnish with whipped topping.

4. Slice remaining banana. Garnish each square with banana slices, chocolate curls, if desired and a strawberry fan. Serve using **Mini-Serving Spatula**.

Yield: 12 servings

Nutrients per serving: Calories 390, Total Fat 17 g, Saturated Fat 6 g, Cholesterol 30 mg, Carbohydrate 52 g, Protein 7 g, Sodium 200 mg, Fiber 3 g

Diabetic exchanges per serving: 2 starch, 1½ fruit, 3 fat (3½ carb)

Wild Raspberry Summer Sipper

Prep time: 10 minutes

This punch sparkles with fizz and fruity flavor. (Pictured on p. 100)

3 cups chilled raspberry-cranberry juice drink

1 quart raspberry sherbet, divided

1 liter (4 cups) chilled lemon-lime flavored carbonated soda

1. Pour juice drink into **Quick-Stir® Pitcher**. Using **Ice Cream Dipper**, pack 2 cups of the sherbet into **Measure-All® Cup**. Add sherbet to pitcher; plunge until well mixed.

2. For each drink, place 1 scoop of the remaining sherbet in 10-ounce drinking glass. Fill glass half full with juice drink mixture (½ cup); add carbonated soda (½ cup) until foam reaches top of glass. Serve immediately.

Yield: 8 servings

Low Fat Nutrients per serving: Calories 210, Total Fat 0 g, Saturated Fat 0 g, Cholesterol 0 mg, Carbohydrate 53 g, Protein 0 g, Sodium 15 mg, Fiber 2 g

Diabetic exchanges per serving: 3½ fruit (3½ carb)

Variation: *Outrageous Orange Summer Sipper:* Substitute orange juice for raspberry-cranberry juice drink and orange sherbet for raspberry sherbet. Proceed as recipe directs.

Cook's Tips

▲ The juice drink and sherbet mixture can be made several hours ahead and refrigerated in the Quick-Stir® Pitcher. Refrigerate any leftover mixture.

▲ Use the Quick-Stir® Pitcher for all of your favorite summertime beverages. The special plunger mixes lemonade, iced tea and powdered drink mixes with just a few pumps of the handle.

Spiced Tropical Tea Cooler

Prep time: 15 minutes   Chill time: 2 hours or overnight

Cool off with a combination of tangy fruit juices mixed with brewed citrus-spice tea.

- **6 cups water, divided**
- **6 tea bags flavored with orange and spice**
- **1 large fresh mint sprig**
- **1 can (12 ounces) frozen orange-peach-mango juice concentrate**
- **¼ cup sugar**
- **Ice cubes**
- **Orange and additional fresh mint (optional)**

1. Bring 4 cups of the water to a boil. Place tea bags and mint in **Classic Batter Bowl**; carefully add boiling water. Let steep 5 minutes. Remove tea bags and mint.

2. Place remaining 2 cups water, juice concentrate and sugar in **Quick-Stir® Pitcher**. Add hot tea; plunge until well mixed. Refrigerate at least 2 hours or overnight.

3. To serve, pour tea mixture into ice-filled glasses. Score orange using **Lemon Zester/Scorer**; cut into thin slices using **Utility Knife**. Garnish iced tea with orange slices and mint, if desired.

Yield: 6 servings

Low Fat Nutrients per serving (1¼ cups): Calories 140, Total Fat 0 g, Saturated Fat 0 g, Cholesterol 0 mg, Carbohydrate 34 g, Protein 1 g, Sodium 40 mg, Fiber 0 g

Diabetic exchanges per serving (1¼ cups): ½ starch, 1½ fruit (2 carb)

Iced Coffee Latte

Prep time: 5 minutes   Chill time: 1 hour

Now you can make tasty gourmet coffee drinks yourself!

- **⅓ cup instant coffee granules**
- **½ cup boiling water**
- **1 can (14 ounces) sweetened condensed milk (not evaporated milk)**
- **2 cups cold water**
- **1 quart cold low-fat chocolate milk**
- **Ice cubes**

1. Place coffee granules in **Small Batter Bowl**. Add boiling water; whisk using **Stainless Steel Whisk**. Whisk in sweetened condensed milk and cold water until completely blended.

2. Pour coffee mixture into **Quick-Stir® Pitcher**. Add chocolate milk; plunge to mix. Chill at least 1 hour. Serve over ice.

Yield: 8 servings

Nutrients per serving (1 cup): Calories 250, Total Fat 4.5 g, Saturated Fat 3 g, Cholesterol 15 mg, Carbohydrate 43 g, Protein 8 g, Sodium 130 mg, Fiber less than 1 g

Diabetic exchanges per serving (1 cup): 3 starch (3 carb)

Cook's Tips

▲ To make *Spiced Berry Tea Cooler*, substitute 1 can (11.5 ounces) frozen cranberry-raspberry juice concentrate for the orange-peach-mango juice concentrate. Proceed as recipe directs.

▲ Regular tea bags, whole cinnamon and cloves can be substituted for the flavored tea bags, if desired. Place 1 cinnamon stick (3 inches), 6 whole cloves and regular tea bags in batter bowl. After steeping, remove cinnamon and cloves along with tea bags and mint. Proceed as recipe directs.

Iced Coffee Latte, Spiced Tropical Tea Cooler,
Wild Raspberry Summer Sipper (p. 99)

Fresh Strawberry Pie

Prep and cook time: 30 minutes   Bake time: 10-12 minutes   Cool time: 30 minutes   Chill time: 4-6 hours

*It's a dream come true for strawberry lovers. This old-fashioned pie
is filled with two pounds of ripe, juicy berries!*

½   **package (15 ounces) refrigerated pie crusts (1 crust)**

2   **containers (1 pound each) fresh strawberries**

½   **cup water**

½   **cup sugar**

2   **tablespoons cornstarch**

1   **lemon**

4   **drops red food coloring (optional)**

1   **cup thawed, frozen whipped topping**

1. Preheat oven to 425°F. Let pie crust stand at room temperature 15 minutes. Gently unfold onto lightly floured surface. Roll to 11½-inch circle using floured **Baker's Roller**™. Place crust in **Deep Dish Pie Plate**, pressing dough into bottom and up sides. Prick bottom and sides using pastry tool. Bake 10-12 minutes or until golden brown. Cool completely.

2. Rinse strawberries in large **Colander**. Remove stems using **Cook's Corer**™. Place 2 cups of the strawberries in **Small (2-qt.) Saucepan**; mash with **Nylon Masher**. Add water and bring to a boil over medium heat. Simmer 2 minutes; strain in small **Colander** over small **Colander Bowl**.

3. Combine sugar and cornstarch. Zest lemon with **Lemon Zester/Scorer** to measure 1 teaspoon zest. Using **Juicer**, juice lemon to measure 1 teaspoon juice. Return strained berry juice to saucepan; discard mashed berries. Using **Nylon Spiral Whisk**, stir sugar mixture, lemon zest and lemon juice into berry juice; bring to a boil over medium heat. Cook 1 minute, stirring constantly, until sauce is clear and thickened. Stir in food coloring, if desired.

4. Slice remaining strawberries with **Egg Slicer Plus**®. Layer half of the sliced berries over bottom of pie crust; spread evenly with half of the sauce. Repeat with remaining berries and sauce. Refrigerate 4-6 hours or until set.

5. To serve, garnish top with whipped topping using **Easy Accent**® **Decorator**. Cut into wedges using **Slice 'N Serve**®.

Yield: 8 servings

Nutrients per serving: Calories 230, Total Fat 9 g,
Saturated Fat 4 g, Cholesterol less than 5 mg, Carbohydrate 36 g,
Protein 2 g, Sodium 100 mg, Fiber 3 g

Diabetic exchanges per serving: 1 starch, 1 fruit, 2 fat (2 carb)

Cook's Tips

▲ For the freshest strawberry pie, use firm, ripe strawberries. Prepare pie earlier in the same day that you plan to serve it. Otherwise, berries tend to become soft and watery, making the filling cloudy.

▲ When placing refrigerated pie crust in the Deep Dish Pie Plate, evenly ruffle edge of crust inside pie plate then firmly press top edge of crust to fluted edge of pie plate in several places.

▲ Do not cover pie when refrigerating until it is completely cooled.

▲ If using a microwave oven without a built-in turntable, rotate cake once after 6 minutes of cooking.

▲ To bake cake in a conventional oven, preheat oven to 325°F. Bake 55-60 minutes or until Cake Tester inserted near center comes out clean. Cool 10 minutes. Invert onto **Stackable Cooling Rack**; remove from pan.

▲ This cake is best when prepared and served the same day.

Sunshine Cake

Prep time: 15 minutes   Microwave time: 11-14 minutes   Stand time: 10 minutes

Breeze through summer with this impressive microwave cake made in our Stoneware Fluted Pan.

- 1 **lemon**
- 1 **orange**
- 1 **small carrot, grated (½ cup)**
- 3 **eggs**
- 1 **container (16 ounces) sour cream**
- 1 **package (18.25 ounces) yellow cake mix**
- ¼ **cup powdered sugar**
  Thawed, frozen whipped topping (optional)
  Lemon and orange wedges (optional)

1. Brush **Stoneware Fluted Pan** with vegetable oil using **Pastry Brush**.

2. Using **Lemon Zester/Scorer**, zest lemon and orange using short strokes. Juice lemon and orange with **Juicer** to measure ¼ cup total juice; set aside. Grate carrot using **Deluxe Cheese Grater**.

3. In **Classic Batter Bowl**, combine eggs, sour cream, carrot, lemon zest and orange zest. Whisk until well blended using **Stainless Steel Whisk**. Add cake mix. Mix until well blended, about 1 minute using **Mix 'N Scraper®**. Pour batter into pan, spreading evenly.

4. Microwave on HIGH 11-14 minutes or until **Cake Tester** inserted in near center comes out clean. (Cake will be slightly moist on top near center.) Let stand in microwave 10 minutes. Loosen cake from sides of pan; invert onto serving plate.

5. Using clean pastry brush, brush reserved citrus juices over top and sides of warm cake. Sprinkle powdered sugar over cake using **Flour/Sugar Shaker**. Cut into slices using **Serrated Bread Knife**. Garnish with whipped topping and lemon and orange wedges, if desired.

Yield: 12 servings

Nutrients per serving: Calories 290, Total Fat 13 g, Saturated Fat 6 g, Cholesterol 85 mg, Carbohydrate 38 g, Protein 5 g, Sodium 320 mg, Fiber less than 1 g

Diabetic exchanges per serving: 2 starch, ½ fruit, 2 fat (2½ carb)

Mile-High Turtle Pie

Prep time: 30 minutes   Freeze time: 4 hours

You will find this delicious ice cream pie, layered with caramel-chocolate sauce and toasted pecans, to be the tastiest way to serve ice cream to a crowd.

1 **jar (12.25 ounces) caramel ice cream topping**

2 **bars (1.55 ounces each) milk chocolate candy, broken into small pieces**

12 **pecan shortbread cookies, finely crushed (1¼ cups crumbs)**

3 **tablespoons butter or margarine, melted**

1 **cup pecan halves, toasted, divided**

1 **container (½ gallon) butter pecan ice cream, divided**

1 **container (½ gallon) chocolate ice cream, divided**

1. In **Small Micro-Cooker®**, combine ice cream topping and chocolate pieces. Microwave on HIGH 1-1½ minutes, stirring every 30 seconds until melted and smooth. Cool slightly.

2. Lightly spray inside of **Springform Pan** with vegetable oil using **Kitchen Spritzer**. Line sides of pan with 2-inch-wide strips of **Parchment Paper**. Place cookies in resealable plastic food storage bag; crush into fine crumbs using **Baker's Roller™**. Place butter in **Small Batter Bowl**; microwave on HIGH 30-45 seconds or until melted. Stir in crumbs. Firmly press crumb mixture onto bottom of pan. Place in freezer.

3. Reserve ½ cup of the toasted pecan halves for top. Coarsely chop remaining pecans using **Food Chopper**. Set aside.

4. Using **Ice Cream Dipper**, scoop half of the butter pecan ice cream over crust, pressing into an even layer. Drizzle with one third of the caramel-chocolate sauce and half of the chopped pecans. Scoop half of the chocolate ice cream over first layer. Drizzle with half of the remaining sauce and sprinkle with remaining chopped pecans. Scoop remaining butter pecan ice cream around edge of pie. Scoop remaining chocolate ice cream in center. Top with reserved pecan halves and drizzle with remaining sauce. Wrap loosely with aluminum foil; place in freezer. Freeze until firm, about 4 hours.

5. Before serving, refrigerate dessert 30 minutes for easier slicing. Release collar from pan; carefully remove paper. Cut dessert into wedges using **Chef's Knife**.

Yield: 16 servings

Nutrients per serving: Calories 660, Total Fat 37 g, Saturated Fat 17 g, Cholesterol 140 mg, Carbohydrate 73 g, Protein 10 g, Sodium 260 mg, Fiber 2 g

Diabetic exchanges per serving: 3 starch, 2 fruit, 6½ fat (5 carb)

Cook's Tips

▲ To toast pecans, preheat oven to 350°F. Spread pecans in a single layer on **Small Bar Pan**. Bake 10-12 minutes or until lightly toasted and fragrant; cool completely.

▲ This dessert can be made and frozen days in advance of serving.

▲ To make cutting this frozen dessert easier, dip the Chef's Knife into warm water and wipe it dry after cutting each wedge.

Hawaiian Dessert Cloud

Prep time: 20 minutes   Freeze time: 6 hours or overnight

Fresh fruit and toasted coconut perfectly complement this creamy frozen dessert shell accented with lime zest and juice.

1   **package (8 ounces) reduced-fat cream cheese (Neufchâtel), softened**

½   **cup sugar**

1   **lime**

1   **container (8 ounces) frozen light whipped topping, thawed**

1   **cup strawberries, sliced**

2   **kiwis, peeled, sliced and cut in half**

1   **mango, cut into ½-inch cubes**

¼   **cup sweetened flaked coconut, toasted**

1. Place **Springform Pan** in freezer. In **Classic Batter Bowl**, mix cream cheese and sugar until well blended.

2. Zest lime with **Lemon Zester/Scorer** to measure 1 teaspoon zest; juice lime with **Juicer** to measure 2 tablespoons juice. Stir zest and juice into cream cheese mixture; mix well. Fold in whipped topping using **Classic Scraper**.

3. Attach open star tip to **Easy Accent® Decorator** and fill with cream cheese mixture. Spread remaining mixture evenly over bottom of chilled springform pan. Pipe a decorative border around bottom, next to collar, to create sides. Cover with aluminum foil; freeze 6 hours or overnight.

4. When ready to serve, hull strawberries using **Cook's Corer™**. Slice strawberries and kiwis with **Egg Slicer Plus®**; place in **Small Batter Bowl**. Gently stir in mango.

5. Place coconut on **Small Bar Pan**. Microwave on HIGH 2-3 minutes until coconut is toasted, stirring every 30 seconds. Run **Quikut Paring Knife** around sides of frozen dessert. Release collar from pan. Fill shell with fruit mixture. Sprinkle with coconut. Cut into wedges using **Slice 'N Serve®** and serve immediately.

Yield: 8 servings

Nutrients per serving: Calories 230, Total Fat 9 g,
Saturated Fat 7 g, Cholesterol 15 mg, Carbohydrate 32 g,
Protein 3 g, Sodium 140 mg, Fiber 1 g

Diabetic exchanges per serving: 1 starch, 1 fruit, 2 fat (2 carb)

Cook's Tips

▲ Refrigerated jarred mango slices, cut into cubes, can be substituted for the fresh mango.

▲ Any combination of sliced and chopped fruits equaling 3 cups can be used for this recipe. Use your favorites!

▲ Once the chocolate
is firm, place treats
between layers of
Parchment Paper in
a tightly covered
container. Store in a
cool place at room
temperature so they
will stay crisp.

▲ The Food Chopper
works well for coarsely
chopping crackers and
cookies.

▲ Use a Twixit! Clip to
secure the bag with the
melted chocolate. This
simple piping bag works
well with icing, too.

Crispy S'more Treats

Prep time: 10 minutes   Cook time: 5 minutes   Cool time: 30 minutes

Even the all-American sweet treat, the s'more, can stand a makeover.
Here, it is transformed into a new fun shape with the Scalloped Bread Tube.

2½   **cups cocoa-flavored sweetened
     rice cereal**

6   **whole (about 5 x 2-inch) graham
     crackers, coarsely chopped**

3   **tablespoons butter or margarine**

2   **tablespoons packed brown sugar**

3½   **cups miniature marshmallows,
     divided**

¾   **cup milk chocolate morsels**

1. Place lid on bottom of **Scalloped Bread Tube**;
   spray with butter-flavored nonstick cooking
   spray. Place cereal in **Classic Batter Bowl**.
   Coarsely chop graham crackers using **Food
   Chopper**; add to cereal and set aside.

2. In **Professional (4-qt.) Casserole**, melt butter
   with brown sugar over low heat, stirring
   occasionally using **Mix 'N Scraper®**. Add
   2½ cups of the marshmallows; stir until
   melted. Remove casserole from heat. Add
   cereal mixture, stir until well coated. Stir in
   remaining 1 cup marshmallows.

3. Using **Large Scoop** sprayed with nonstick
   cooking spray, immediately place a few scoops
   of cereal mixture in bread tube; press mixture
   evenly with **Tart Shaper**. Repeat to fill bread
   tube. Cool completely.

4. Remove lid from bread tube. Push mixture out
   onto **Cutting Board**; cut crosswise into ½-inch
   slices using **Serrated Bread Knife**.

5. Microwave chocolate morsels in **Small
   Micro-Cooker®**, uncovered, on HIGH
   1 minute, stirring every 15 seconds, until
   chocolate is melted and smooth. Pour
   chocolate into small resealable plastic food
   storage bag; twist top of bag and secure. Cut
   a small tip off corner of bag. Decorate treats
   with chocolate; let stand until set.

Yield: 16 treats

Nutrients per serving (1 treat): Calories 140, Total Fat 5 g,
Saturated Fat 3 g, Cholesterol 10 mg, Carbohydrate 24 g,
Protein less than 1 g, Sodium 100 mg, Fiber 0 g

Diabetic exchanges per serving (1 treat): 1½ fruit, 1 fat (1½ carb)

Lemon Blueberry Cheesecake Torte

Prep time: 30 minutes   Bake time: 15-18 minutes   Chill time: 1 hour

This stunning triple-layered cake is full of refreshing lemon flavor and a rich, creamy cheesecake filling.

1 **package (16 ounces) pound cake mix (plus ingredients to make cake)**

1 **large lemon**

¾ **cup boiling water**

1 **package (6 ounces) lemon gelatin**

1 **package (8 ounces) cream cheese, softened**

⅓ **cup cold milk**

1 **container (12 ounces) frozen whipped topping, thawed**

1 **package (3.4 ounces) cheesecake instant pudding and pie filling**

1 **kiwi, peeled, sliced and cut in half**

1 **cup blueberries**

Lemon slices and fresh mint (optional)

1. Preheat oven to 400°F. Line **Stoneware Bar Pan** with 13-inch piece of **Parchment Paper**. Prepare cake mix according to package directions; pour into pan, spreading evenly. Bake 15-18 minutes or until **Cake Tester** inserted in center comes out clean; cool 10 minutes. Using edges of paper, carefully lift cake onto **Stackable Cooling Rack**; cool completely.

2. Zest lemon using **Lemon Zester/Scorer**; set aside. Juice lemon using **Juicer** to measure ¼ cup juice. Pour boiling water into **Small Batter Bowl**. Add gelatin and 2 tablespoons of the juice; reserve remaining juice for cream cheese mixture. Stir until gelatin is dissolved.

3. Invert cooled cake onto smooth side of **Large Grooved Cutting Board**; remove paper. Prick cake at ½-inch intervals using **Hold 'N Slice™**. Using **Pastry Brush**, brush cake evenly with all but 2 tablespoons of the gelatin mixture. Trim ¼ inch around edge of cake; discard edges. Cut cake crosswise into 3 equal layers.

4. In **Classic Batter Bowl**, combine cream cheese and remaining 2 tablespoons lemon juice; whisk until smooth. Add milk; whisk until smooth. Spoon whipped topping over cream cheese mixture. (Do not mix.) Sprinkle with pudding mix; mix well using **Classic Scraper** until smooth. (Mixture will be thick.)

5. Place 1 cake layer on **Oval Platter**. Attach open star tip to **Easy Accent® Decorator**; fill with filling mixture. Pipe a straight border around edge of cake layer. Using **Large Scoop**, place 4 scoops of filling down center; spread evenly to border. Top with second cake layer. Repeat filling as above. For third layer, pipe a decorative border around edge. Spread any remaining filling down center.

6. Arrange kiwi slices on top of cake. Add blueberries to reserved gelatin mixture; mix gently. (If gelatin mixture has set, microwave on HIGH 5-10 seconds or until softened.) Spoon blueberries over top of cake; sprinkle with reserved zest. Garnish with lemon slices and mint leaves, if desired.

Yield: 16 servings

Nutrients per serving: Calories 320, Total Fat 14 g, Saturated Fat 7 g, Cholesterol 45 mg, Protein 5 g, Carbohydrate 43 g, Sodium 290 mg, Fiber 0 g

Diabetic exchanges per serving: 2 starch, 1 fruit, 2 fat (3 carb)

Cook's Tips

▲ Slicing a peeled kiwi is easy using the **Egg Slicer Plus®**. Open and place the kiwi crosswise in slicer and slice through it with wires.

▲ For ease in serving, slice the torte with the **Serrated Bread Knife** and serve using **Mini-Serving Spatula**.

▲ To prepare scored lemon slices, begin by scoring lemon at ½-inch intervals using the **Lemon Zester/Scorer**; cut lemon into thin slices.

▲ This dessert can be assembled and refrigerated several hours in advance. Be sure to keep the dessert well chilled.

Cook's Tips

▲ When placing refrigerated pie crust in the Deep Dish Pie Plate, evenly ruffle edge of crust inside pie plate for picture-perfect results. To keep crust from slipping down sides of pie plate, firmly press edge of pie crust to fluted edge of pie plate in several places.

▲ To soften cream cheese, microwave on HIGH 30 seconds.

▲ Use the Ice Cream Dipper to easily scoop the sherbet. It contains a food-safe de-icing solution that warms from the heat of your hand while you are scooping. This unique solution allows for easy release of the sherbet from the dipper.

▲ This pie can be made 1 day before serving. Store covered in the refrigerator.

Prep time: 30 minutes Bake time: 10-12 minutes Cool time: 30 minutes Chill time: 1 hour

The refreshing flavor and delicate texture of this citrus pie make it especially appealing after a hearty meal.

½ **package (15 ounces) refrigerated pie crust (1 crust)**
1 **medium orange**
1 **package (8 ounces) cream cheese, softened**
½ **cup boiling water**
1 **package (3 ounces) orange gelatin**
3 **cups orange sherbet, divided**
1 **container (8 ounces) frozen whipped topping, thawed, divided**
   Additional orange for garnish

1. Preheat oven to 425°F. Let pie crust stand at room temperature 15 minutes. Gently unfold onto lightly floured surface. Roll to 11½-inch circle using floured **Baker's Roller™**. Place crust in **Deep Dish Pie Plate**, pressing dough into bottom and up sides. Prick bottom and sides using pastry tool. Bake 10-12 minutes or until golden brown. Cool completely.

2. Using **Lemon/Zester Scorer**, zest orange to measure 1 teaspoon zest; juice orange with **Juicer** to measure ¼ cup juice. Place cream cheese in **Classic Batter Bowl**; whisk juice and zest into cream cheese until smooth using **Stainless Steel Whisk**.

3. Microwave water in **Small Micro-Cooker®** on HIGH 1½-2 minutes or until boiling. Whisk in gelatin and stir 2 minutes until completely dissolved. Using **Ice Cream Dipper**, pack 1 cup of the sherbet into **Measure-All® Cup**; gradually add to gelatin, stirring until mixture is well blended and thickened. Immediately whisk gelatin mixture into cream cheese mixture in batter bowl.

4. Add half of the whipped topping (1½ cups) to cream cheese mixture; mix gently until well blended using **Mix 'N Scraper®**. Fill pie shell with filling. Chill at least 1 hour.

5. Fill **Easy Accent® Decorator** with remaining whipped topping. Score additional orange for garnish; cut 2 slices using **Utility Knife**, then cut each slice into quarters. Cut pie into wedges using **Slice 'N Serve®**. Garnish each serving with whipped topping, a scoop of remaining orange sherbet and quartered orange slice.

Yield: 8 servings

Nutrients per serving: Calories 570, Total Fat 31 g, Saturated Fat 18 g, Cholesterol 45 mg, Carbohydrate 66 g, Protein 6 g, Sodium 350 mg, Fiber 0 g

Diabetic exchanges per serving: 2½ fruit, 2 starch, 6 fat (4½ carb)

Candy Bar Parfaits

Prep time: 15 minutes

Kids will love making their own candy and ice cream sensations any day of the week.

I   **bar (1.55 ounces) milk chocolate candy, coarsely chopped**

⅓   **cup chocolate-flavored syrup**

2   **tablespoons creamy peanut butter**

I   **cup mini-twist pretzels, coarsely chopped**

¼   **cup peanuts, coarsely chopped**

I   **quart vanilla ice cream**

4   **(10-ounce) clear plastic drinking glasses**

Additional mini-twist pretzels and peanuts (optional)

1. Place candy bar in freezer 5 minutes for easier chopping. Meanwhile, in **Small Batter Bowl**, whisk together syrup and peanut butter using **Stainless Steel Whisk**; set aside.

2. Using **Food Chopper**, coarsely chop candy bar, pretzels and peanuts; combine in small bowl.

3. To assemble parfaits, use **Ice Cream Dipper** to place 1 scoop ice cream in each of 4 drinking glasses. Top each with one fourth of the candy bar mixture and second scoop of ice cream. Top with chocolate sauce and garnish with additional pretzels and peanuts, if desired. Serve immediately.

Yield: 4 servings

Nutrients per serving: Calories 510, Total Fat 26 g, Saturated Fat 12 g, Cholesterol 60 mg, Carbohydrate 64 g, Protein 11 g, Sodium 380 mg, Fiber 2 g

Diabetic exchanges per serving: 4 starch, 4 fat (4 carb)

Cook's Tips

▲ To make parfaits ahead of time, assemble as recipe directs except do not top with chocolate sauce. Place parfaits covered in freezer. When ready to serve, top with sauce and garnish, if desired.

▲ Vanilla frozen yogurt can be substituted for the vanilla ice cream, if desired. This lighter version has 15 grams less fat and 50 milligrams less cholesterol than the original parfait.

▲ Any favorite candy bar, chocolate-covered pretzels or chocolate-dipped peanuts can be used in this simple ice cream treat.

▲ Four large apples can be substituted for the 6 medium apples. You need about 2 pounds of apples for this recipe.

▲ There's no need to thaw the mixed berries. If strawberries are large, cut them in half.

▲ Ground cinnamon can be substituted for the Korintje Cinnamon, if desired.

▲ To prepare this dessert in a conventional oven, preheat oven to 375°F. Prepare topping as recipe directs except do not microwave. Spoon fruit filling into Square Baker and sprinkle with topping. Bake 40-45 minutes or until apples are tender.

Apple Berry Crisp

Prep time: 30 minutes   Microwave time: 20-22 minutes   Stand time: 30 minutes

This is a classic comfort food, updated with microwave directions to keep the kitchen cool.

Topping

- ¼ **cup butter or margarine, melted**
- ¼ **cup chopped almonds, pecans or walnuts**
- 1½ **cups old-fashioned or quick oats**
- ⅓ **cup packed brown sugar**
- ½ **teaspoon** *Pantry Korintje Cinnamon*

Fruit Filling

- 6 **medium Granny Smith apples**
- 1 **lemon**
- 1 **package (12 ounces) frozen unsweetened mixed berries**
- ⅓ **cup granulated sugar**
- 2 **tablespoons all-purpose flour**
- ½ **teaspoon** *Pantry Korintje Cinnamon*
  Vanilla ice cream (optional)

1. For topping, microwave butter in **Large Micro-Cooker®** on HIGH 45-60 seconds or until melted. Chop nuts using **Food Chopper**. Add nuts, oats, brown sugar and cinnamon to melted butter; mix well. Microwave 3 minutes or until browned and bubbly, stirring halfway through cooking time. Pour mixture out onto sheet of **Parchment Paper**; cool.

2. For fruit filling, peel, core and slice apples using **Apple Peeler/Corer/Slicer**. Cut apples in half using **Utility Knife**. Separate slices into large **Colander Bowl**. Zest lemon using **Lemon Zester/Scorer** to measure ½ teaspoon zest. Juice lemon using **Juicer** to measure 2 teaspoons juice. Add berries, zest and juice to bowl; toss gently using **Mix 'N Scraper®**. In small **Colander Bowl**, combine granulated sugar, flour and cinnamon. Add to apple mixture; toss to coat evenly.

3. Spoon apple mixture into **Square Baker**. Microwave on HIGH 14-16 minutes or until apples are tender, turning baker after 8 minutes. Sprinkle with topping. Continue microwaving 2 minutes. Let stand at least 30 minutes. Serve warm or at room temperature with vanilla ice cream, if desired.

Yield: 8 servings

Nutrients per serving: Calories 280, Total Fat 9 g, Saturated Fat 4 g, Cholesterol 15 mg, Carbohydrate 48 g, Protein 4 g, Sodium 60 mg, Fiber 6 g

Diabetic exchanges per serving: 1 starch, 2 fruit, 1 fat (3 carb)

Bananas Foster Stir-Fry

Prep time: 10 minutes   Cook time: 5 minutes

This classic dessert sauce has been around forever,
but never as easy (or as light) as our fabulous version!

5   **medium bananas**

1   **lemon**

1   **jar (12.25 ounces) fat-free caramel
     ice cream topping**

½   **teaspoon *Pantry Korintje Cinnamon***

1   **teaspoon rum extract**

1   **quart frozen vanilla low-fat yogurt
     or ice cream**

1. Slice bananas using **Egg Slicer Plus®**. Zest lemon using **Lemon Zester/Scorer** and juice lemon with **Juicer** to measure ¼ cup juice.

2. Combine ice cream topping, lemon juice and cinnamon in **Stir-Fry Skillet**. Bring to a boil over medium-high heat, stirring occasionally; remove from heat. Gently stir in bananas and rum extract; toss gently using **Small Mix 'N Scraper®**.

3. For each serving, spoon about ⅓ cup of the banana mixture over frozen yogurt scooped with **Ice Cream Dipper**. Garnish with lemon zest.

Yield: 8 servings

Nutrients per serving: Calories 370, Total Fat 4 g,
Saturated Fat 2 g, Cholesterol 50 mg, Carbohydrate 74 g,
Protein 11 g, Sodium 150 mg, Fiber 2 g

Diabetic exchanges per serving: 5 starch (5 carb)

Cook's Tip

▲ Try *Bananas Foster Stir-Fry* served over toasted pound cake. Heat **Professional Grill Pan** over medium-high heat 5 minutes. Place pound cake slices in pan; toast 30 seconds on each side or until grill marks appear.

▲ To toast almonds,
spread almonds in a
single layer in **Small Bar
Pan**. Bake at 350°F for
10-12 minutes or until
golden brown. Cool
completely. The
almonds can be toasted
at the same time as the
cookie is being baked.

▲ Instead of
using pre-melted
unsweetened chocolate
flavor, you can
substitute 2 squares
(1 ounce each)
unsweetened chocolate
for baking. Place
squares in Classic
Batter Bowl; microwave
uncovered on HIGH
45 seconds, stirring
every 15 seconds, until
melted and smooth.
Add crumbled cookie
dough to batter bowl
and proceed as recipe
directs.

▲ This recipe can be
made and refrigerated
up to 8 hours in
advance.

Double Chocolate Cherry Dessert Pizza

Prep time: 30 minutes   Bake time: 12-14 minutes   Cool time: 1 hour   Chill time: 2 hours

*When chocolate and cherries team up, the result is usually
dramatic and delicious. This recipe is no exception.*

1　**package (18 ounces) refrigerated
　　chocolate chip cookie dough**

2　**packets (1 ounce each) pre-melted
　　unsweetened chocolate flavor**

1　**package (8 ounces) cream cheese,
　　softened**

¼　**cup powdered sugar**

1　**tablespoon milk**

½　**teaspoon almond extract**

1　**container (8 ounces) frozen whipped
　　topping, thawed, divided**

1　**can (21 ounces) cherry pie filling**

¼　**cup sliced natural almonds, toasted**

1. Preheat oven to 350°F. Crumble cookie dough
into **Classic Batter Bowl**. Add chocolate flavor;
stir with **Bamboo Spoon** until thoroughly
blended.

2. Shape cookie dough into a ball in center of
Large Round Stone. Using lightly floured
Baker's Roller™, roll out dough to 11½-inch
circle, about ¼ inch thick. Bake 12-14 minutes
or until edges of cookie are set and center is
no longer moist. (Cookie will be soft. Do not
overbake.) Remove baking stone to **Stackable
Cooling Rack**. Cool cookie 10 minutes.
Carefully loosen cookie from baking stone
using **Serrated Bread Knife**; cool completely
on baking stone.

3. In **Small Batter Bowl**, mix cream cheese,
powdered sugar, milk and almond extract until
well blended. Attach open star tip to **Easy
Accent® Decorator**; fill with whipped topping.
Fold remaining whipped topping into cream
cheese mixture.

4. Spread cream cheese mixture over cooled
cookie to within ½ inch of edge using **Large
Spreader**. Spoon pie filling over cream cheese.
Pipe 16 whipped topping rosettes evenly
around outside edge. Garnish with any
remaining whipped topping. Sprinkle with
almonds. Refrigerate 2 hours. Cut into wedges
using **Slice 'N Serve®**.

Yield: 16 servings

Nutrients per serving: Calories 320, Total Fat 18 g,
Saturated Fat 9 g, Cholesterol 20 mg, Carbohydrate 35 g,
Protein 3 g, Sodium 150 mg, Fiber 2 g

Diabetic exchanges per serving: 2 starch, 3 fat (2 carb)

Grilled Peach Melba Dessert

Prep time: 15 minutes   Cook time: 8-17 minutes

Sweet endings can be guilt-free, too. Angel food cake slices get a light toasting in our Professional Grill Pan before being topped with grilled fresh peaches, raspberry sauce and vanilla ice cream in this de-light-ful dessert.

4   **firm, ripe medium peaches**
1   **teaspoon fresh lemon juice**
8   **slices (1 ounce each) angel food cake**
1½ **teaspoons butter or margarine**
½   **cup light, sugar-free red raspberry preserves**
2   **tablespoons hot water**
1   **cup vanilla ice cream**
¾   **cup raspberries**
    Mint leaves (optional)

1. Cut each peach into 6 wedges using **Utility Knife**. Place in **Classic Batter Bowl**. Sprinkle with lemon juice; toss gently and set aside.

2. Heat **Professional Grill Pan** over medium heat 5 minutes. Place half of the cake slices in pan, pressing gently onto bottom. Toast 1-3 minutes on each side or until lightly toasted using **Nylon Tongs** to turn. Repeat with remaining cake slices.

3. Add butter to pan; use **Pastry Brush** to spread melted butter. Add peaches; cook 4-5 minutes, turning once. Remove pan from heat. In **Small Batter Bowl**, mix preserves and water.

4. To assemble dessert, place 1 cake slice and 3 peach wedges on each of 8 dessert plates. Drizzle raspberry sauce over peaches. Top cake with scoop of ice cream using **Medium Scoop**. Sprinkle with raspberries. Garnish with mint, if desired.

Yield: 8 servings

Low Fat   Nutrients per serving: Calories 150, Total Fat 3 g, Saturated Fat 2 g, Cholesterol 9 mg, Carbohydrate 33 g, Protein 3 g, Sodium 230 mg, Fiber 2 g

Diabetic exchanges per serving: 1 starch, 1 fruit (2 carb)

Cook's Tips

▲ Once peaches have been tossed with the lemon juice, you can let them stand up to 1 hour before grilling and they won't discolor.

▲ If you prefer, peaches can be peeled. To remove skins, bring 1 quart water to boil in **Small (2-qt.) Saucepan**. Carefully lower peaches into water using **Nylon Slotted Server**. Remove peaches after 1 minute and plunge into bowl of cold water. Pull off skins with **Paring Knife**.

▲ Purchase a baked angel food cake from the bakery section of the supermarket and you'll keep your kitchen cool while getting a quick start to this easy dessert. Cut angel food cake with a gentle sawing motion using the **Serrated Bread Knife**.

Index

About Our Recipes

All recipes were developed and tested in The Pampered Chef Test Kitchens by professional home economists. For best results, we recommend you use the ingredients indicated in the recipe. The preparation and cooking times at the beginning of each recipe serve as a helpful guide when planning your time in the kitchen. As an important first step, we suggest you read through the recipe and assemble the necessary ingredients and equipment. "Prep time" is the approximate amount of time needed to prepare recipe ingredients before a final "Cook time." Prep time includes active steps such as chopping and mixing. It can also include cooking ingredients for a recipe that is assembled and then baked. Some preparation steps can be done simultaneously or during cooking and are usually indicated by the term "meanwhile." Some recipes that have steps not easily separated have a combined "Prep and cook time."

Notes on Nutrition

The nutrition information in *Casual Cooking* can help you decide how specific recipes can fit into your overall meal plan. At the end of each recipe, we list calories, total fat, saturated fat, cholesterol, carbohydrate, protein, sodium, and fiber. We also include diabetic exchange information commonly used by people with diabetes. This information is based on the 1995 Exchange Lists for Meal Planning by the American Diabetes Association and the American Dietetic Association. For each recipe, two lists of exchanges are provided. The first option is based on the traditional method of figuring diabetic exchanges; the second option is given in parentheses and reflects the newer system of carbohydrate counting. If you use the exchanges, consult your doctor, certified diabetes educator or registered dietitian.

Nutritional analysis for each recipe is based on the first ingredient listed whenever a choice is given and does not include optional ingredients, garnishes, fat used to grease pans, or serving suggestions. The ingredients used in our recipes and for nutritional analyses are based on most commonly purchased foods and unless indicated otherwise use 2 percent reduced-fat milk and large eggs. Recipes requiring ground beef are analyzed based on 80-90 percent lean ground beef. Recipes requiring ground turkey are analyzed based on 93 percent lean ground turkey. When margarine is an ingredient option, use a product containing 80 percent fat and not vegetable oil spread. Recipes labeled as **Low Fat** have 3 grams or less fat per serving.

Metric Conversion Chart

Volume Measurements (dry)	Volume Measurements (fluid)	Dimensions
1/8 teaspoon = 0.6 mL	1 fluid ounce (2 tablespoons) = 30 mL	1/8 inch = 3 mm
1/4 teaspoon = 1.25 mL	4 fluid ounces (1/2 cup) = 125 mL	1/4 inch = 6 mm
1/2 teaspoon = 2.5 mL	8 fluid ounces (1 cup) = 250 mL	1/2 inch = 1 cm
3/4 teaspoon = 3.75 mL	12 fluid ounces (1 1/2 cups) = 375 mL	3/4 inch = 2 cm
1 teaspoon = 5 mL	16 fluid ounces (2 cups) = 500 mL	1 inch = 2.5 cm
1 tablespoon = 15 mL		
2 tablespoons = 30 mL	**Weights (mass)**	**Oven Temperatures**
1/4 cup = 50 mL		250°F = 120°C
1/3 cup = 75 mL	1 ounce = 30 g	275°F = 140°C
1/2 cup = 125 mL	4 ounces = 125 g	300°F = 150°C
2/3 cup = 150 mL	8 ounces = 250 g	325°F = 160°C
3/4 cup = 175 mL	12 ounces = 350 g	350°F = 180°C
1 cup = 250 mL	16 ounces = 1 pound = 500 g	375°F = 190°C
		400°F = 200°C
Recipes in this cookbook have not been tested using metric measures. When converting and preparing recipes with metric measures, some variations in quality may be noticed.		425°F = 220°C
		450°F = 230°C